ROYAL BIRMINGHAM
CONSERVATOIRE

ROYAL BIRMINGHAM CONSERVATOIRE

INSPIRING MUSICIANS SINCE 1886

CHRISTOPHER MORLEY

First published 2017 by
Elliott and Thompson Limited
27 John Street, London WC1N 2BX
www.eandtbooks.com

ISBN: 978-1-78396-319-5

Picture Credits:
Dennis Assinder: page 39; Sam Bagnall: page 208; Birmingham Conservatoire
Archive: pages 32, 33, 47, 55, 74; Birmingham and Midland Institute: pages 42,
43; Graeme Braidwood: front cover and pages 18, 19, 23, 26, 101, 102, 103, 112, 113,
116, 117, 131, 141, 142/3, 144, 145, 147 (right), 151, 152, 154, 173, 175, 176, 180, 181 188, 189,
190, 191, 192, 193, 194, 195, 196, 197; William Ellis: pages 22, 150, 155, 164, 165, 167,
178, 209; Feilden Clegg Bradley: pages 76, 78, 79, 81, 82, 83; Michael Nicholson
/ Getty Images: page 35; Simon Hall: page 147 (left); Stephen Ibbs: page 34;
Lebrecht Music & Arts: page 37; Dylan Line: pages 25, 63, 179; Greg Milner
photography: back cover and pages 1, 6, 12, 13, 14, 15, 16, 17, 20, 21, 29, 49, 50, 86,
89, 90, 98, 126, 129, 132, 148, 153, 158, 159, 160, 161, 162, 170, 171, 172, 174, 177, 183, 211,
212, 213, 219; Christian Payne: pages 135, 166, 168, 169; Millie Pilkington: page 10,
© 2013 The Royal Household Bagshot Park; Tom Oxley: page 105; Nick Robinson:
pages 87, 182; Aimee Spink: pages 2, 109, 210, 121, 122, 123; Stuart Targett: pages
114, 115, 118, 119; Thousand Word Media: page 9; Tom White/CBSO: page 72; Alan
Wood: pages 156, 157; www.chriswebbphotography.com: pages: 58/9, 84/5, 136,
149; Tan Yuchen: pages 205, 206

9 8 7 6 5 4 3 2 1

A catalogue record for this book is available from the British Library.

Design by Karin Fremer

Printed in China by 1010 Printing Group Ltd

Front cover image: A performance of Stockhausen's *Der Kleine Harlekin*.
Back cover image: The final concert at the Adrian Boult Hall, June 2016.
Preceding and following pages: These striking images demonstrate the
richness and variety of performance at the Conservatoire.

David Brock's *The Birmingham School of Music: Its First Century* was published (in a shabbier format than it deserved, it has to be said) by the City of Birmingham Polytechnic in the centenary year of 1986. The book is meticulously researched and beautifully written – as one would expect from a postgraduate in Professor Anthony Lewis's Music Department of the University of Birmingham, where David and I first met. It is a goldmine of information that no subsequent historian of the Birmingham School of Music/Birmingham Conservatoire can afford to ignore.

Over Indian meals and snooker, David and I became close friends in 1966. Three years later I was his best man when he married Evelyn, and it was thanks to David (by then Vice-Principal at the BSM) that I was invited to teach Paperwork at the School of Music, which was how my time on the staff there began.

When Julian Lloyd Webber asked me to write this new history, my thoughts immediately flew to David, and how invaluable his own history would prove to me.

I dedicate this book with gratitude and affection to his memory.

CONTENTS

Preface

In September 2017 Birmingham Conservatoire began the most exciting chapter in its long and colourful history when it opened its doors to a brand new, state-of-the-art, fully digital music college with a new and intensely significant name: the Royal Birmingham Conservatoire. Purpose-built for the needs of the twenty-first century and embracing both music and acting, its students will enjoy unrivalled facilities in addition to five public performance spaces.

It is a wonderful and remarkable time to be Principal and we are looking forward to grasping this unique opportunity with both hands. It is vital that we 'get it right' both for the future of music education in the United Kingdom and for the city of Birmingham itself. We want to repay this unprecedented and far-sighted investment by Birmingham City University with a Conservatoire that is central to the life of this great city. Music has the power to bring people together – it knows no barriers of language, race or background. A twenty-first-century music college must recognise this and reach out to all. That is why our outreach programme – which aims to discover and nurture talent from across the UK – will be at the centre of what we do. And our digital facilities will mean we can deliver our teaching programmes in real time across the world.

Christopher Morley's timely book reveals the trials, tribulations and triumphs the Conservatoire has experienced along the way to reaching this exalted moment in its history. It makes fascinating reading.

Professor Julian Lloyd Webber
Principal, Royal Birmingham Conservatoire

Professor Julian Lloyd Webber, Principal.

Foreword

How does the Royal Birmingham Conservatoire distinguish itself from all the others? Well of course it's the people who have passed through its doors, whether they are students or staff. The building, the performance spaces, the practice rooms are important and many will remember fondly particular occasions, but it is people and performances which bring the spaces alive.

Christopher Morley's book provides a fascinating chronicle of the Royal Birmingham Conservatoire's history from its earliest beginnings as the Birmingham School of Music nearly a century and a half ago. There is a part of it devoted to the various homes the Conservatoire has occupied and looks forward to its new home, the United Kingdom's first purpose-built music college for a generation.

However, what really sets this book apart are the characters, starting with the Principals who, it seems, had varying degrees of success in the role. Then there are the various music departments, from the obvious to the perhaps not quite so obvious, but beautifully illustrated by a fantastic library of photographs of students. Although it is the selection of 'Recollections' by individuals that probably best sum up the life and value of the Conservatoire.

Apart from acknowledging Christopher Morley's excellent research, what I think he should be congratulated on is making this book feel that it is more about the future. The past is merely the foundation for the next stage, where unrivalled facilities can inspire students to greater achievements. Enhancing Birmingham's reputation as a vibrant centre in the world of music can only lead to wider recognition and appreciation. It is those ideas of what is possible next which comes through the pages of this book, which I'm sure we all hope will be an exciting and successful future for the Royal Birmingham Conservatoire.

Edward

HRH The Earl of Wessex, KG GCVO
Patron, Royal Birmingham Conservatoire

Birmingham Conservatoire is a musical kaleidoscope,
with a wide variety of recitals, solo performers and opera productions.

INTRODUCTION

When the then Birmingham School of Music celebrated its official centenary in 1986 it had come a long way from the loosely organised singing classes offered as part of the outreach of the Birmingham and Midland Institute in the middle of the nineteenth century. By 1986 it had become a major faculty of the City of Birmingham Polytechnic, which on 16 June 1992 achieved university status as the University of Central England. Later, the Music Department, rechristened the Birmingham Conservatoire, found itself under the banner of what had now become Birmingham City University.

During the three decades since the publication of its last official history, the institution that is now Birmingham Conservatoire has experienced much and undergone many spectacular transformations.

Departments have been expanded; new ones have been created; exciting new courses aspiring to ever higher degrees of excellence have appeared; the recruitment of staff now draws from a far more starry and international pool than in the centenary year of 1986, and student numbers have grown exponentially, again with an invigorating international input. The profile of the Conservatoire has become a huge presence in the cultural life of its home city, and there have also been hands reaching across oceans and frontiers to form valuable and beneficial links with similar institutions worldwide, including those in the United States, Hungary and Singapore.

As members of the Conservatoire, students have enjoyed and benefited from its strong connections with the City of Birmingham Symphony Orchestra and with the UK's greatest concert hall – arguably one of the world's greatest concert venues – in the form of Symphony Hall, as stewards, backstage helpers or page-turners.

Though Birmingham's musical cognoscenti have always been aware of the School of Music's activities, it was perhaps not until the opening of the Paradise Place building by Her Majesty Queen Elizabeth The Queen Mother in 1973 and Simon Rattle's acceptance of its Presidency a few years later (something he devotedly maintains to this day, with Peter Donohoe alongside him as Vice President), that the institution permeated the greater public consciousness. Now there is a sense of pride in the Conservatoire, obviously boosted by the presence of Julian Lloyd Webber as Principal, just as there is in the awareness of the internationally renowned CBSO under the exciting music directorship of Mirga Gražinytė-Tyla at Symphony Hall. It is good to know that the already well-established links

OPPOSITE, AND FOLLOWING PAGES Conservatoire students hard at work.

between the Conservatoire and the CBSO are set to be strengthened by the bond that has developed between these two personalities.

The School of Music developed within the Birmingham and Midland Institute, as it continued to do when it was moved under the governance of the City of Birmingham Education Department, and eventually, as Birmingham Conservatoire, when it became a faculty of Birmingham City University. This book draws attention to some of the underlying tensions that occasionally beset these relationships, and celebrates the happy outcome that prevails today.

The current relationship between the Conservatoire and BCU is a healthy and supportive one – indeed, it is to that relationship that we owe the building of the magnificent new state-of-the-art home in which the Conservatoire now proudly finds itself, on the splendid campus that has been created on previously derelict, now rejuvenated, brownfield land within which the BCU has relocated all its constituent colleges.

Felix Mendelssohn was fortunate when he founded the role model for subsequent conservatoires in Leipzig in 1843; it was funded by a generous grant from the Kingdom of Saxony, and was financially beholden to no one. And it was Mendelssohn's conception of what a conservatoire should be that continues to inform the Conservatoire in Birmingham: a passing down of the greatest standards of musicianship from current musicians to the next generation. The emphasis in Mendelssohn's day was on orchestral music – in Leipzig, the ancient Gewandhaus orchestra provided the tutors; in Birmingham, it is the players of the remarkable City of Birmingham Symphony Orchestra – but nowadays horizons are far wider.

The concept remains, though. Something as unique as a college whose aim is to educate each individual student to achieve the highest standards of musicianship needs the freedom to be untrammelled, perhaps even to be idiosyncratic, as it forms its own character. It needs to be a little apart from the routine of the running of less volatile departments, and the augurs are that Birmingham City University acknowledges and welcomes the public awareness that the world-encompassing presence of the Conservatoire brings to the parent institution.

A major part of this book is devoted to an account of the various Principals who have presided over the activities of the School of Music and the Birmingham Conservatoire, some of whom have made more of a lastingly successful contribution than others. The current Principal is Julian Lloyd Webber, whose expertise in the professional field as a world-famous cellist and whose passion for musical education are second to none.

His appointment in 2015 coincided with the announcement of the Conservatoire's move into a new building; the two events created what Elgar claimed for his First Symphony: 'a massive hope for the future'. It is Julian I have to thank for his vision in commissioning this book.

When I attended a reunion of staff and students at Birmingham Conservatoire in June 2016, my name badge reminded me that I had taught at the Conservatoire for twenty-two years, between 1988 and 2010 (theory, music history, aural, keyboard skills, performance and liberal studies – a course I and the students, after their initial reluctance, really enjoyed sharing). But my chief activity was, and still is, reviewing musical events as chief music critic of the *Birmingham Post* – so I have experienced the Conservatoire's activities from both viewpoints.

In preparing this book I circulated a questionnaire to alumni and past members of staff. Many fascinating replies came back, some brief and to the point, some absorbingly detailed and expansive, as you will read here.

During the course of my reviewing activities it is my constant pleasure to bump into past students from my near quarter-century of teaching at Birmingham Conservatoire, as they perform with the CBSO, Stratford-upon-Avon's Orchestra of the Swan, Welsh National Opera, Longborough Festival Opera, and even beyond these shores. They all love talking about their time as students in Birmingham, and look forward to reading all about their beloved Conservatoire – its history, its anecdotes, its triumphs – within the pages of this book.

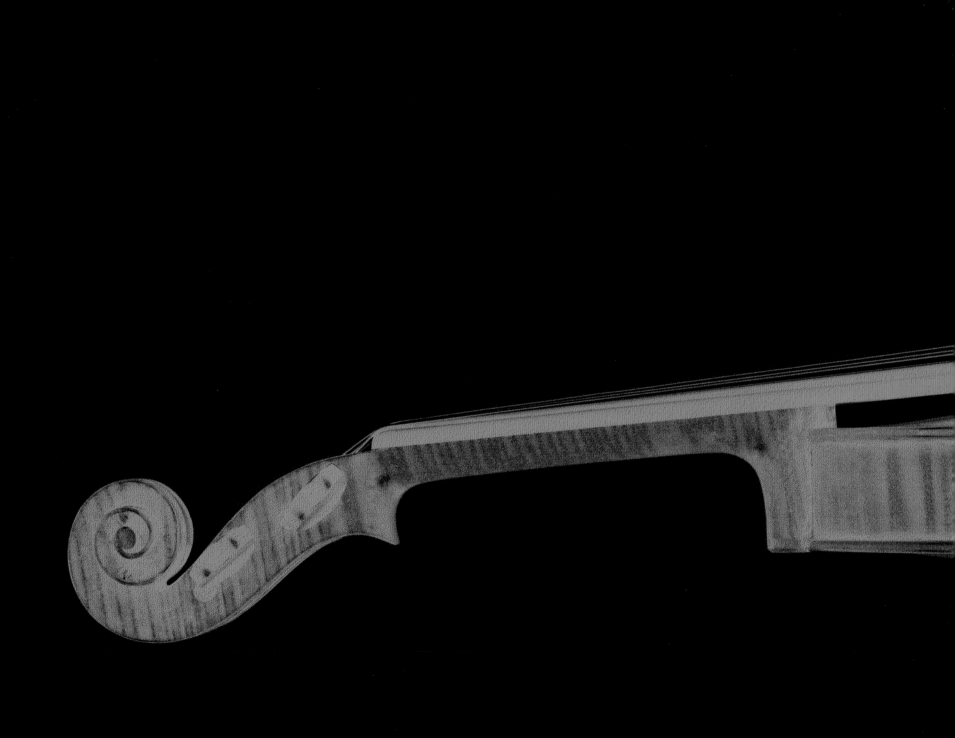

1 THE STORY OF BIRMINGHAM CONSERVATOIRE

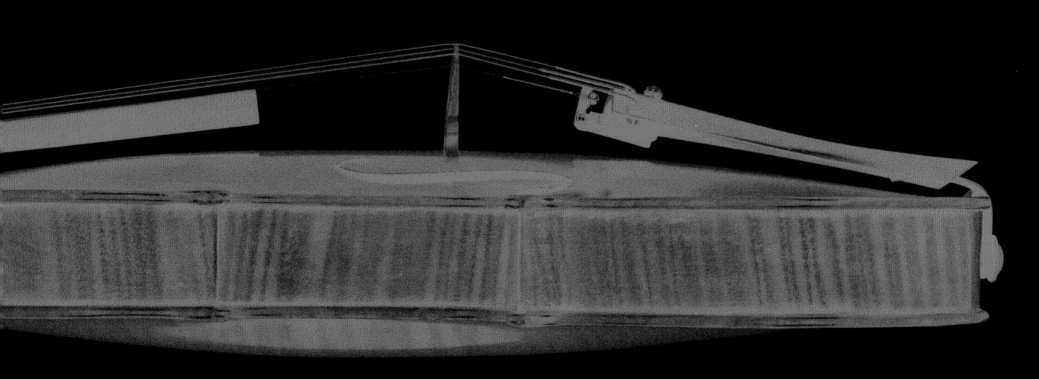

The Birmingham and Midland Institute was the original home of the Birmingham School of Music, proudly situated on Paradise Street, just opposite Birmingham Town Hall.

On 12 May 1989, immediately after Birmingham School of Music changed its name to Birmingham Conservatoire, the office telephone was ringing red-hot, receiving calls enquiring about veranda extensions, or with questions concerning the Tory party. It was to take some time before the penny dropped, when people began to realise that the name 'conservatoire' implied an institution where the highest musical values were taught and maintained, under the tuition of highly accomplished performers.

It was fitting that the inspiring example of the Leipzig Conservatorium, founded by Felix Mendelssohn, with its professors drawn from that city's Gewandhaus orchestra, should be followed in Birmingham, where the composer had been such a favourite visitor and premiered his great oratorio *Elijah*, with a Conservatoire many of whose teachers were drawn from the ranks of the City of Birmingham Symphony Orchestra.

The puzzling word had in fact been used nearly a century earlier, in the September 1900 issue of the Birmingham and Midland Institute magazine, which had entertained great hopes for the success of the composer Granville Bantock as recently appointed Principal of the School of Music, 'in connection with our conservatoire'.

Her Majesty Queen Elizabeth The Queen Mother arriving in Paradise Street for the opening of the first phase of the new building of Birmingham School of Music in 1973. Ironically, this was just around the corner from its original home within the BMI.

But we are jumping the gun. There is quite a history, dating from the second half of the nineteenth century, before we can reach the important arrival of Granville Bantock.

Born out of the worthy aim of self-improvement for the working man, who had been servicing the success of the Industrial Revolution since the late 1700s, the Birmingham and Midland Institute opened its doors in 1854 in a handsome building on land granted by Birmingham Town Council adjacent to Birmingham Town Hall. It 'combined in one body an Industrial Department designed to provide part-time classes for scientific instruction with a General Department designed on the lines of a literary and philosophical institution'.

Birmingham had long boasted a fine tradition of choral singing, centred on the Triennial Musical Festival launched in 1784 to raise funds for the General Hospital, and it was with a vocal class that the first inklings of a School of Music established a foothold. Alfred J. Sutton, conductor of the Amateur Harmonic Association, undertook a class of Elementary Instruction in Singing in the summer term of 1859, but the already small number of students dwindled from the outset, and it folded two years later.

GRANVILLE BANTOCK

Born in London in 1868, Granville Bantock was originally destined for a career in the Indian Civil Service, but instead became a brilliant student at the Royal Academy of Music, where several of his early works were performed.

After leaving the Royal Academy of Music in 1893 Bantock spent an extensive period as a conductor, showing a great sympathy for the music of his fellow contemporary English composers, not least in his programming of concerts at The Tower, New Brighton. Among the luminaries he invited to conduct their own works there were Parry, Stanford and Elgar ('*Enigma' Variations*). Elgar dedicated his *Pomp and Circumstance March* No. 2 to 'my friend Granville Bantock'. Bantock was also generous in his support of foreign composers, not least of Sibelius, who at that time was still relatively unknown outside his native Finland. Sibelius dedicated his Third Symphony to Bantock, and accepted his invitation to conduct the UK premiere of his Fourth Symphony at the Birmingham Triennial Musical Festival in 1912.

Bantock himself was a prolific composer. His works often showed an interest in the Orient – in which he nearly found a career as a diplomat – not least in the huge *Omar Khayyám* trilogy for voices and orchestra. He was knighted in 1930, and retired from both the Birmingham School of Music and the University of Birmingham in 1934. Towards the end of his life, having left his Harborne home in Birmingham and returned to London, he turned to making piano arrangements of well-loved works for domestic consumption. He died in 1946.

Sir Edward Elgar   Prof. Granville Bantock

The elegant entrance hall of the School of Music's temporary home in the old YMCA, later the Midlands Electricity Board building in Birmingham's Dale End.

But in 1863 a Mr Richard Rickard, a mathematics teacher at King Edward's School, persuaded the BMI Council to allow him to open a Penny Class in Elementary Singing, which proved so popular (by the autumn of 1874 the average attendance was 543) that branch classes were launched elsewhere in the suburbs. And then came a crucial step in the direction of the establishment of a more professional attitude towards music teaching in the Institute's Industrial Department, with the appointment in 1877 of Alfred R. Gaul to take a class in The Theory of Music.

Gaul, conductor of the Birmingham Sunday School Choral Union, had already achieved success the previous year with the premiere of his *Silent Land* at the Birmingham Triennial Musical Festival, and his engagement now was a major step in the eventual establishment of a school of music. Classes in piano, solo singing for ladies, 'clarionet', flute, cello and part-singing were added in 1885, and a year later the whole enterprise was brought under an official umbrella with the appointment of William Stockley as Honorary Principal.

So it was that 1886 marked the birth of the Birmingham School of Music, still under the auspices of the Birmingham and Midland Institute – something that would lead to increasing tensions down the following decades – but now with a sense of its own identity.

Stockley was a decidedly big noise in Birmingham musical circles. He had been conductor of the Birmingham Festival Choral Society since 1855, rescuing what had been at that time a moribund institution, and also ran his own series of orchestral concerts.

He assembled around him a staff of fourteen, among them Frederick Ward, who taught viola and orchestral studies. Fred Ward played among the violins in 'Stockley's Band', during which time he performed Dvořák's Sixth Symphony under the composer's baton on 21 October 1886. His desk partner on that occasion was none other than Edward Elgar, who composed his violin piece *La Capricieuse*, Op. 17, in 1891 for Ward.

Classes proliferated, with the addition of other woodwind and orchestral instruments, and even organ tuition. But various issues stood in the way of the BSM's aspirations to be considered the equal of the London colleges, and the desire to award qualifications that would carry the same weight as certificates from those establishments.

In 1894 Ebenezer Prout – yes, we university undergraduates in the 1960s used to sing words to Bach's G minor Fugue, BWV 578, lampooning him for his name, but we should have gone down on our knees

A pen-and-ink sketch of Birmingham by Felix Mendelssohn. The picture was originally sketched on a letter he wrote from London, dated 2 October 1840.

Facsimile of a pen-and-ink sketch by Mendelssohn in the possession of Mr. Felix Moscheles, and reproduced by his kind permission.

to him as certainly a more brilliant musician than any of us – commented unfavourably on the custom of teaching in classes those subjects which ought to be taught on an individual basis.

This proved a wake-up call to what had perhaps become a complacently sleepy institution, and more teachers were engaged. One of the results was the end of collective classes in Solo Singing (just think about that as a ridiculous concept).

A more significant outcome was the appointment in 1900 of one of the country's most thrusting, aware and receptive composers and conductors, Granville Bantock, as a salaried Principal. Stockley, for all his influence, was stuck in the remembered glories of his prime, half a century earlier. (Also in 1900, Stockley's old-fashioned rehearsal methods and responses had been the cause of the choral collapse – the tenors dropping in pitch in the unaccompanied passage early on – at the premiere of Elgar's *Dream of Gerontius* at the Triennial Festival.) It was time for things to move on.

The Annual Report of the BMI in 1900 stated that:

'The Council hope that they have found in Mr Granville Bantock one who will realise their long-cherished hopes. He comes with the highest recommendations from Sir Alexander Mackenzie, Sir John Stainer, Sir Hubert Parry, Dr [Charles] Villiers Stanford, and other eminent authorities. He has entered upon his work with enthusiasm; he is organising a Students' Choir and Orchestra, holding fortnightly rehearsals in the Large Lecture Theatre, and is transforming the School from a number of unconnected classes into an organised School.'

A high accolade came in 1902, when Edward Elgar accepted an invitation from the Council to accept the appointment of Honorary Visitor to the School, replying:

'I feel very much honoured by the invitation of the Council of the Midland Institute to accept the post of visitor in connection with the School of Music: this I do with very great pleasure, as I trust it will be a means of my helping local music, and being associated with Mr Granville Bantock, for whom, as you well know, I have the highest admiration and esteem.'

In fact the mutual regard held between Elgar and Bantock was to come to spectacular fruition a few years later. A gun had virtually been held at Elgar's head to accept the newly created Professorship of Music at the University of Birmingham, funded – on condition that the appointment should be offered and taken up by Elgar – by the great Birmingham musical philanthropist Richard Peyton. One can scarcely imagine the social climber Elgar, well balanced with a chip on both shoulders, being dragged kicking and

The High Victorian terracotta exterior of the temporary Dale End home at the far end of Birmingham city centre, and not too far from the new Eastside site.

DR ALLEN K. BLACKALL

Dr Allen K. Blackall had been appointed to the School of Music in 1918, teaching Harmony and Counterpoint, and Advanced Theory of Music. He had been involved with the Birmingham Festival Choral Society as assistant chorus master since 1904, working successively under Dr G. R. Sinclair (immortalised in Elgar's *'Enigma' Variations)*, Sir Thomas Beecham and Sir Henry Wood.

screaming to the Chair, nor picture his wife Alice wringing her hands in grief, but his tenure did not last long.

Elgar's Professorship began in 1905 with an inaugural lecture at the School of Music within the BMI. As with the others that followed, this was hard-hitting, and often kicking at the shins of the British musical Establishment, but Elgar had no wish to keep this up for ever. Behind the scenes, he was quietly building up the foundations of what was to become a great Department of Music, not least in ordering important items for the library, including the complete works of Henry Purcell. But in 1908, obviously needing to free himself from the shackles of academic administration in order to devote himself entirely to composition, he resigned.

The Peyton Chair of Music had been established, and Elgar's successor was announced on 4 November 1908: Granville Bantock, combining in one person the headships of two fledgling organisations – the Birmingham School of Music and the Music Department at the University of Birmingham – and fulfilling Elgar's hope that 'the School of Music may prove the practical training ground for his students. He believes there is no reason why the Birmingham School of Music at the Midland Institute should not some day rival the older institutions in Manchester and London,' as a special correspondent had written in the *Birmingham Post* four years earlier.

Bantock's appointment as Head of both the Birmingham School of Music and the Department of Music at the University of Birmingham provided the cement for a relationship that still flourishes today, with a heartening interaction between both establishments (as this author remembers, making the weekly pilgrimage between the University's Edgbaston campus, to which the Department of Music had eventually removed, and Dale End in the city centre for piano lessons at the BSM with the despairing Janice Williams between 1966 and 1969).

Much had been achieved during the more than third of a century that Bantock had been Principal of the BSM, including the launch of operatic activity, even if on a somewhat rocky basis.

But there were also stresses and cracks becoming apparent between the School of Music and the Birmingham and Midland Institute, of which the BSM remained technically and constitutionally a mere department, subject to the dictates of the BMI Council. These tensions would continue for many decades as the BSM struggled to achieve autonomy for itself as a national – and indeed international

– institution, aspiring to provide musical education at the highest level, only to be dragged down by insular politics.

Even as early as 1903, after he had been Principal for only three years, Bantock was at odds with his nominal employers. Apparently there had been complaints about his methods, and he replied accordingly:

'At all times I have endeavoured to treat the teachers and students with consideration. In certain cases I may have been obliged to exercise the authority to which I considered myself entitled as Principal . . . for the general welfare, order and development of the School.

'At no time have I either publicly or in an official capacity ever disparaged the great classical masters. I need only point to the Examination Syllabus and to the Concert Programmes to show that I place the greatest value on classical works and their educational worth . . . but advocate a need for progress.'

Written in an intimidatingly firm hand, Bantock's letter continues with rebuttals as to his use of the orchestra to provide accompaniments instead of performing in its own right ('A student orchestra, as I conceive it, is formed for study and not for display, and the practise of accompaniments affords

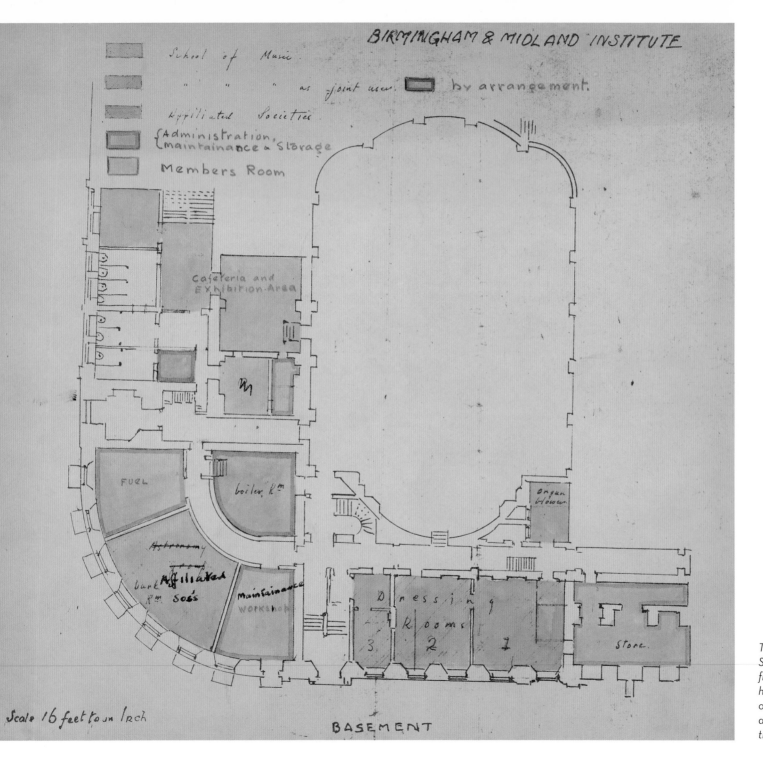

BIRMINGHAM & MIDLAND INSTITUTE

School of Music.

" " " as joint user. by arrangement.

Affiliated Societies

{ Administration,
{ maintainance & Storage

Members Room

Cafeteria and
Exhibition Area

FUEL

boiler Rm

Organ
blower

Astronomy

Affiliated
Socs

Maintainance
WORKSHOP

Dressing
Rooms
3   2   1

Store.

Scale 16 feet to an Inch

BASEMENT

The original ground plans of the School of Music, unearthed in 2016 from the archives of the Birmingham and Midland Institute. It was obvious that great importance was attached to the establishment of the BSM within the BMI.

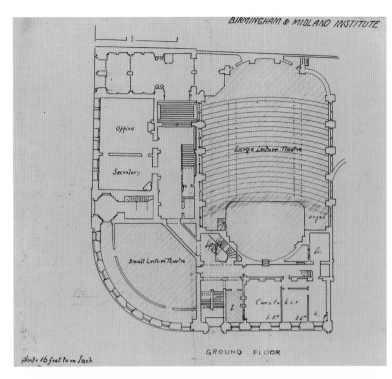

Office

Secretary

Large Lecture Theatre

Organ

Small Lecture Theatre

Caretaker

Scale 16 feet to an Inch

GROUND FLOOR

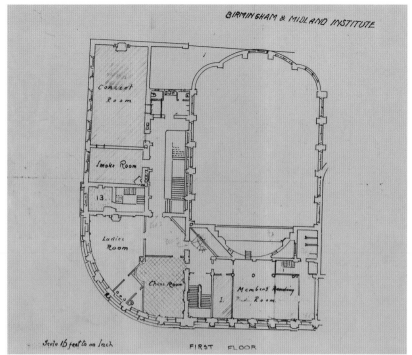

Concert Room

Smoke Room

13

Ladies Room

Chess Room

Members Reading Room

Scale 16 feet to an Inch

FIRST FLOOR

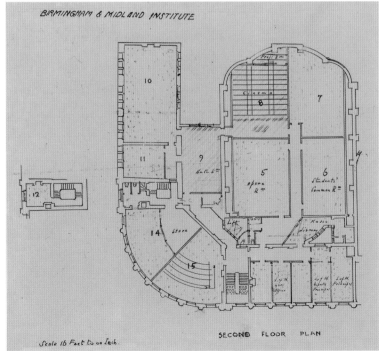

10

Cinema 8

7

11

9

5 Common Rm

6 Students' Common Rm

14

Store

15

12

Scale 16 Feet to an Inch.

SECOND FLOOR PLAN

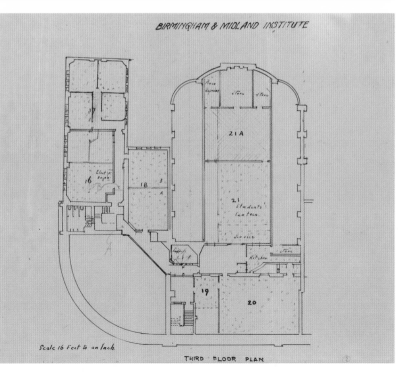

16

18

21 A

21 Students' Canteen

Kitchen

19

20

Scale 16 Feet to an Inch

THIRD FLOOR PLAN

excellent discipline'); a strong assertion, when Ivor Atkins, organist of Worcester Cathedral, was proposed by Elgar to take his place as Visiting Examiner, of the importance of demetropolisation that carries even more weight today ('concerning which I am strongly of opinion that the Provinces should be able to assert their independence of the Capital in musical matters'). There were other, more technical, complaints to which Bantock provided robust answers, and he concluded with a huge, swirling signature.

The Chairman of the BMI wrung his hands:

'Dear Sir, The Committee have come to the conclusion that there is no substantial grievance: and they earnestly appeal to the complainants, in their own interests, as well as for the good of the School, to co-operate loyally and cheerfully with the Principal, of whose ability and devotion to the welfare of the School the committee are firmly convinced, and thus render his difficult task as agreeable to himself and themselves as possible.

Yours faithfully,

Chairman.'

Note, no 'Dear Mr Bantock', nor no name in the sign-off. The rifts had begun to open. Bantock's vision was too much for some of the amateurs (and indeed some of the staff) at the Birmingham School of Music, who thought they could have an easy ride for their money at the BSM, and was bewildering for the hierarchy at the Birmingham and Midland Institute. The tensions between the School of Music and the BMI would only get worse down the decades until a mutual release became possible.

Bantock's successor as Principal, Allen Blackall, one-time organist of St Mary's Church in Warwick and chorus master of the Birmingham Festival Choral Society, appointed largely as a result of the lobbying carried out by his fellow staff members at the Birmingham School of Music, was busy trying to consolidate the fortunes of the opera class. He felt that it 'had become too large and therefore impossible to manage. It was much too open for anybody and everybody to come along and claim membership. The effort to find something for everybody to do met with failure largely owing to the very irregular attendance of a few to whom important roles had been assigned.'

His solutions involved a pragmatic choice of work to consider the limitations of staging and casting, a requirement for the singers to be regular in attendance and be note- and word-perfect 'by the stated time, thereby facilitating the producer's task', and the stipulations that there was to be no easy ride – membership of the class was to be for one production only and there was to be no guarantee of automatic inclusion in subsequent presentations.

This move towards a professionalism of attitude indicated that the School of Music was growing beyond the worthy amateurism of the parent Birmingham and Midland Institute, and the cracks between the two were becoming ever more apparent.

Having seen the School of Music through the doldrums of the war years, Blackall resigned in 1945, to be replaced by Christopher Edmunds, who had joined the staff in 1929. Well known locally as an organist and composer, Edmunds had the enthusiastic support of his colleagues, and set about rebuilding the spirit and depleted membership of the School of Music.

An early and important development during his time as Principal was the establishment of the GBSM diploma in 1946, a qualification that enhanced the status of the School nationally. Edmunds also presided over moves that consolidated the financial security of the teaching staff, and took steps to monitor the quality of students, making the application process more rigorous and thereby ensuring that the BSM met the standards required by the City of Birmingham Education Authority as it contemplated the establishment of a specialist music school for

STEUART WILSON

Steuart Wilson, despite losing a lung and a kidney during the First World War, had been a much sought-after singer, working closely with, among others, Ralph Vaughan Williams. Apart from his appearances as a performer, he had a most glittering career as Musical Director of the Arts Council, newly formed in the wake of the Second World War; Head of Music for the BBC (though he refused to own a radio); Deputy Administrator of the Royal Opera House, Covent Garden, and as an overseas examiner for the Trinity College of Music.

There was, however, some extra-curricular notoriety. Wilson had successfully sued the BBC for publication in its esteemed *Listener* weekly magazine of a letter from someone criticising his vocal production in a broadcast performance of Bach's *St Matthew Passion*. Nowadays any artist would make themselves a laughing stock for such defensiveness. His boorish and predatory behaviour had driven his wife into the arms of Adrian Boult, no less. Boult, despite Wilson in his BBC role compelling him to resign as conductor of the BBC Symphony Orchestra as soon as he reached the age of sixty, had urged the Birmingham School of Music to appoint Wilson as its new Principal.

Most spectacularly, as a result of his experiences fighting against what he perceived as a gay mafia at the Royal Opera House, Wilson published a pamphlet declaring that all homosexuals should be excluded from working in the arts. Presumably he would have banned all works by Tchaikovsky, Tippett, Britten, Menotti and Barber (and that's just for a start) from the Opera House repertoire.

under-16s planning subsequent entry to an accredited college of music.

Certainly it was thanks to the determination with which Christopher Edmunds set about strengthening the status of his department that the Birmingham and Midland Institute in February 1949 gave belated recognition to its significance, officially acknowledging the title 'Birmingham School of Music', though stipulating that it should appear beneath the BMI heading on official papers.

Edmunds's period as Principal was characterised both by a generous concern for the creation of a positive working environment for the benefit of students and staff within a professionally constituted establishment and also by the continually deteriorating relationship with the parent BMI. Lack of co-operation – perhaps even deliberate sabotage – from above had a detrimental effect on the morale of staff and students. Edmunds's resignation came in 1956. Despite an overwhelming petition from the staff for his reinstatement, the Institute Council felt this would not be in the School's best interest. One could comment that it was perhaps the attitude of the Institute itself that was not in the School's best interest.

There was a school of thought that, given there were no full-time members of staff, there was no need for a full-time Principal, so why not appoint an actively performing musician as a figurehead? Instead, have a full-time administrative officer to support the work of this trophy flag-waver. Allan Bixter was appointed to this newly created post, while the great Midlands-born pianist Denis Matthews, a soloist frequently appearing with the CBSO, was head-hunted to become the next Principal.

For some reason Matthews's proposed appointment created a furore, and he withdrew his interest. The *Birmingham Post* summarised the situation:

'The former full-time Principal of the Birmingham School of Music resigned in July last year because of a policy clash with the council of the Birmingham and Midland Institute.'

Mr Denis Matthews was appointed the new Principal on, it was understood, a one-day-a-week basis, while the committee of enquiry was investigating the resignation of Dr Edmunds.

Following controversy over his appointment, including protests about its part-time nature, Mr Matthews withdrew his acceptance of the post. At the same time he said that if the controversial issues could be settled he would be willing to receive a renewed offer of the post.

The official opening by the Duchess of Gloucester of the Adrian Boult Hall on 20 February 1986. After performances by CBSO Wind Ensembles conducted by Okku Kamu, the orchestra's principal guest conductor, the concert ended with the premiere of The Marshes of Glynn *by BSM head of composition Andrew Downes (centre on the podium). To his right is BSM director of studies Damian Cranmer, who conducted the BSM Symphony Orchestra and Chorus, and to his left is tenor soloist John Mitchinson.*

The issues, whatever they were, remained unsettled, so the BSM was deprived of what would have been a glamorous if perhaps rocky Principalship. (Denis Matthews eventually became professor of music at the University of Newcastle-upon-Tyne from 1971 to 1984.) Bad publicity over this entire farrago resulted in the warning off of many possible candidates, until at last the renowned tenor Sir Steuart Wilson accepted the appointment, with perhaps the most controversial consequences.

Wilson's short stint as Principal was not without incident. He might have had the attribute of not suffering fools gladly, but he also had the knack of putting his own foot in things. On one occasion he brought his golden cocker spaniel Argo into the canteen (there are conflicting reports as to whether the animal actually performed on the premises); on another he spilt ink over his trousers and removed them before sitting doggedly behind his desk as he interviewed a prospective student and his parents.

More seriously, he uxoriously attempted to involve his wife Mary, who was not on the staff, in the running of the School of Music. Without advertising and interviewing for the post, he appointed her as a cello teacher, provoking the BMI's School of Music

'Wilson's short stint as Principal was not without incident. He might have had the attribute of not suffering fools gladly, but he also had the knack of putting his own foot in things.'

OPPOSITE AND OVERLEAF
Two students of brass instruments.

Committee to instruct him to remove her. Wilson refused, and attempted to get her into the BSM instead as a student of the harp.

This ploy was rejected by the committee, and Wilson put the whole matter into the hands of his solicitors, to which the BMI responded by deciding that 'in view of the general attitude of the Principal during recent months, any further suggestion of a compromise was not worth pursuing. It therefore recommends that the Principal be dismissed.' The resolution was carried by the chairman's casting vote, but eventually more moderate voices prevailed, and the dismissal resolution was rescinded, thus allowing Lady Wilson to raise her head again.

This time it was over the issue of the redecoration of the ladies' lavatory. According to Margaret Stewart, who succeeded Mary as Wilson's third wife, the Principal was asked by the foreman to suggest a colour scheme, and Wilson naturally turned to his consort for advice. This was deemed yet another case of 'Lady Wilson interfering'. Angry minutes followed and 'a more appropriate colour scheme' was chosen. We shall never know what decor had been suggested by the lady.

Evidently the huge clash of personalities between Wilson and Eric Knight, secretary of the Birmingham and Midland Institute, was due to end in collision. Eventually the matter became public when the Revd R. G. Lunt, Chief Master of King Edward's School, and a Governor of the Institute, addressed a meeting of the City Education Committee in February 1960, as the *Birmingham Post* reported:

'It has been for a long time now that I have kept these troubles under my hat. I have been terribly shocked at the government – or rather the misgovernment – of the School of Music.

'Today I am driven to using strong words, but they are considered words. I feel pretty strongly about these things, having been through some 18 months of misery and frustration . . .

'I have been driven to the conclusion that the leadership of the Institute just tolerates the School of Music and does so only for the sake of the money it brings in. And that is a tidy sum: £13,000 a year for the management of the school.

'Here I think is a unique cultural and educational feature of this great city . . . it is in a sorry state, moribund, riddled by intrigue and run by internal manipulation preferring hole and corner methods to the light . . .

'The present Principal has done much good to the cause of musical education in the Midlands. This summer he comes to the end of his appointed term. It has been good for us in Birmingham to have had him even for a short time.'

Letters poured into the paper, including from Wilson himself, who also penned one to *The Times*, which had taken an interest in the scandals. Wilson asked the BMI to grant him early release from his contract, so that he could go on an examining tour of India, to which the Council agreed, adding a note of 'appreciation of his services to music in the city during his period of Principalship'.

It was only a few years after this fiasco that responsibility for the Birmingham School of Music passed in 1965 from the Birmingham and Midland Institute to the Birmingham City Council's Further Education Committee and, as we shall see elsewhere, that coincided with a move to separate homes, one comfortably permanent for the BMI (where it still remains at the time of writing), the other thankfully temporary for the BSM.

Meanwhile, another singer was appointed as the next Principal of the School of Music. This was the distinguished baritone Gordon Clinton, recommended by the composer Sir George Dyson, one-time Director of the Royal College of Music, as 'the sort of man to put the place on its feet'.

Which it certainly needed, and not just as a result of the Wilson debacles. There were currently fewer than forty full-time students, not one of them a singer, and Clinton himself described the orchestra as 'absolutely diabolical'. Various authorities warned that the School was struggling to survive, and that it needed to take stock.

Clinton set about doing that very thing: he improved the library; he appointed Frank Downes, a horn-player with the CBSO, to sort out the orchestra, and a new opera school was founded, with the renowned bass David Franklin as production director and Allan Bixter in charge of the music. Changes were made to the teaching syllabus, bringing courses into line with new Ministry of Education plans.

But though the volume of applications for admission increased, the standard of the students was too often of poor musical quality, and a weeding-out process was instigated, resulting in the loss of between fifty and sixty students 'of a very low calibre'.

The stocktaking worked, resulting in a favourable assessment of the School in 1962, but then came the huge upheaval of a search for new premises when plans for a new layout of Birmingham city centre necessitated the demolition of the magnificent Midland Institute building, as well as the adjacent

Central Library. Gordon Clinton calmly oversaw the search for a new home, and supervised the eventual settling into what had formerly been Midland Electricity Board offices in Dale End, at the opposite fringe of the city centre.

Here the environment was far from ideal – not least with demolition work going on next door, creating constantly intrusive noise, and causing styluses to judder on LP records during lectures – but the regeneration of the School of Music continued regardless.

And plans were well under way for a return to the city centre, with a purpose-built new home in Paradise Circus. The move into these new premises came about at roughly the same time as perhaps Gordon Clinton's greatest gift to posterity, his creation in 1973 of the City of Birmingham Symphony Orchestra Chorus.

He and Louis Frémaux, the CBSO's dashing French Principal Conductor, set up a choir dedicated to performing hand in glove with the orchestra and subscribing to the highest professional standards. (Previously concerts had been given with choruses independent in their own right.) Auditions were stiff, and there was a compulsory retirement age of forty-five. This was a premature waste of accumulated wisdom and experience and has since been dropped, but regular auditions for serving members remain rigorously exacting. Today the CBSO Chorus under director Simon Halsey is one of the world's top amateur choral ensembles, much in demand all over the globe, with a top-class reputation.

Having achieved both these goals, Gordon Clinton resigned as Principal at the end of the 1972–73 session, leaving as his legacy a School of Music that had grown under his tenure from thirty-eight full-time students to nearly two hundred.

Clinton was succeeded as Principal by John Bishop, previously Director of Studies, but soon obliged to resign from this demanding figurehead position through ill-health. Bishop became instead Tutor for Admissions, instigating an applicant-friendly auditioning process appreciated as much by those who failed their entry procedure as by those who succeeded.

Louis Carus, Head of Strings at the Royal Scottish Academy, was appointed Principal of the BSM. He presided genially and assiduously over the School of Music's settling into its new home; he forged links with European organisations, and under his guidance a thriving, performance-driven Department of Composition was established under composer Andrew Downes.

LOUIS CARUS

Louis Carus was Principal when the School of Music at last acquired its much needed main concert room, the Adrian Boult Hall, opened by the Duchess of Gloucester on 20 February 1986. This was to become the rehearsal venue for the City of Birmingham Symphony Orchestra, which now also had administrative offices elsewhere in the School of Music building, so the students had the benefit and stimulus of rubbing shoulders with some of the greatest orchestral musicians in the world – and even with the CBSO's Principal Conductor, Simon Rattle.

For all Louis Carus's hands-on, caring attitude towards his charges at the Birmingham School of Music, he could also be not quite of this world and forgetful, as Helen Mills, alumna, widow of the much loved academic lecturer Anthony Cross, and now a driving force in the Birmingham Conservatoire Association, recalls:

'I do remember that Louis periodically had us in individually to play to him in his office, presumably so he could evaluate the general standard . . . He came across as slightly bumbling and a little eccentric to us students but I think that, in his own way, he got things done. Latterly, I do remember Tony coming home from work saying that he had been seen disappearing out of the building with his fiddle under his arm off to do a gig when there were foreign dignitaries due to meet him. I think that sort of thing happened a few times, but my feeling is that the standard at the college definitely moved up and on during his time as Principal.'

Louis Carus was followed as Principal in 1987 by Roy Wales, vastly experienced as a choral trainer, and whose previous positions included Director of Music at the University of Warwick and at the Conservatorium in Queensland. Wales had the distinction of conducting both the UK and Australian

This rather Brutalist frontage onto Paradise Circus remained anonymous for many years until at last the actual identification was added. It was occasionally used for sponsored abseiling attempts.

premieres of Leonard Bernstein's huge, multi-faceted *Mass*, with the composer's approval.

Wales was determined to sharpen up the efficiency of the School of Music, which he certainly had the experience to implement. I once witnessed him publicly rebuking two wet-behind-the-ears freshers who were sniggering at an important, much respected guest speaker welcoming them to the institution; 'more power to his elbow' were my thoughts as an ex-schoolteacher.

But he fell out with the authorities at the City of Birmingham Polytechnic, under whose umbrella the School of Music now sheltered, and he left abruptly. Richard Silk, Director of Studies, surveying his own career at the Birmingham School of Music and Conservatoire, hints tantalisingly at the difficulties:

'I lived through six Heads/Principals. Despite their faults, all left something positive. Clinton guided the early development with the Polytechnic; Louis Carus helped to establish the Adrian Boult Hall, having previously bought for the Recital Hall a second-hand carpet which was fire-damaged with singed bits, and which added to the general effect; Roy Wales persuaded us that we needed to market the place in a modern way; Kevin Thompson steadied the ship after the debacle of the aforementioned RW;

and George Caird raised the profile of the college to a new level and extended its influence internationally.'

Silk also rescued a forthcoming Birmingham Town Hall performance of Elgar's *Dream of Gerontius* by BSM forces following, in Silk's words, 'Roy Wales's sudden departure'.

Meanwhile a major naming issue was under way. By the late 1980s, it was felt that 'Birmingham School of Music' was beginning to sound provincial and unambitious. Birmingham followed the example of its twin city of Leipzig (at the time still part of East Germany, secreted behind the Iron Curtain), where Birmingham's favourite adopted son Felix Mendelssohn had founded a Conservatorium in 1848, and renamed its centre of musical excellence 'Birmingham Conservatoire'. The re-christening was carried out during a visit by the eminent composer Sir Michael Tippett in 1989.

Roy Wales was succeeded by Kevin Thompson, a hugely experienced professional trumpeter, and an amiable personality perfectly suited to rescue the Conservatoire from the mire that was threatening to submerge it yet again. Under Thompson's guidance, the Conservatoire began to test its toes in international waters, as well as reasserting itself as a major college of choice within this country.

Thompson recalls:

'It was a time when Birmingham was going through a cultural renaissance, with Simon Rattle at the CBSO, the glimmerings of Symphony Hall, Sadler's Wells coming to the city as the Birmingham Royal Ballet . . . I'd been educated in European conservatoires, and I thought we should bring that kind of ethos to Birmingham. We did get various brickbats in the early days from conservative diehards.'

Thompson's tenure (1989–93) was surprisingly short, and some of that period involved a sabbatical at the Crane School of Music in New York, during which Stewart Buchanan, a non-musician senior staff member at the University of Central England, proved a wonderfully efficient and sympathetic stand-in Principal. Kevin Thompson went on to become Director at Dartington College in Devon, and is currently Master of University of Macau Moon Chun Memorial College in Southeast Asia.

The appointment of George Caird, previously Head of Woodwind and Orchestral Studies at the Royal Academy of Music in London, as Principal heralded what was probably one of the most significant periods in the history of what was now the proudly proclaimed Birmingham Conservatoire. He held the office until 2010. Caird, a much admired

KEVIN THOMPSON

In June 2017 Kevin Thompson was appointed Knight of the National Order of the Legion of Honour for his outstanding contribution to French music, arts and culture.

Determined by a decree from the French President, the National Order of the Legion of Honour is awarded to individuals with 'outstanding merit acquired in the service of France in a civilian or military capacity'.

Former recipients of the 'Légion d'honneur' include tenor Plácido Domingo, writers Graham Greene and J. K. Rowling, actress Kristin Scott Thomas, film director Wong Kar-Wai and Nobel Laureates Ang San Suu Kyi, Joseph Stiglitz and Seamus Heaney.

Conservatoire forces await the arrival of alumnus Michael Seal to conduct them in Benjamin Britten's War Requiem in Birmingham Town Hall on 1 July 2011.

oboist, and with strong family connections in the musical world, was able to consolidate the Conservatoire's place in the international world (particularly establishing links in China and Singapore, as well as in Russia and Eastern Europe). He also maintained his own performing career, not least at prestigious concerts within the Adrian Boult Hall (a wonderful account of Mozart's *Gran Partita*, к. 361, under Caird's direction remains in the memory), and his diplomatic skills smoothed over whatever tensions were simmering.

During Caird's time as Principal, the Birmingham Conservatoire's parent, the University of Central England, changed its name to Birmingham City University, and moves were afoot to transfer all the faculties to Birmingham Eastside. All well and good, but Caird had fears for the autonomy and financial independence of what had now become the Music Department of BCU.

'George resigned on a matter of principle after long disagreements with Vice Chancellor David Tidmarsh over the future of the Conservatoire,' Jeremy Patterson of the Birmingham Conservatoire Association remembers.

'Tidmarsh got his way and subsumed the Conservatoire into a much larger faculty, presumably with a view to making it into a university music department. George argued that a higher-education college of music is a different animal and has a different ethos, needing the flexibility to secure financial support from other sources, such as HEFCE [the Higher Education Funding Council for England], in order to respond to staffing needs. Julian Pike said in his address at George's retirement party that he was the most successful Principal of all UK music colleges. I understand that George turned down the opportunity to be Principal of the Royal Academy of Music, which would probably have led to a knighthood, as he very much wanted to stay with the Conservatoire.

'Tidmarsh put an end to that, which is to be greatly regretted. Many of us are angry and unforgiving. The similarities with Doctor Edmunds are striking.'

Peter Johnson, who retired as Head of Research in 1990, recounts the struggles he had in consolidating the academic aspect of study at the Conservatoire:

'In 1990, when I arrived, the Conservatoire was in deep trouble. The undergraduate course (GBSM) was losing students at a rate of around 30 per cent and the course had twice failed its validation and was hence technically invalid. I was appointed to rethink the GBSM from scratch and to reverse the trend.

Within one year the attrition rate fell to about 2 per cent, partly by simply listening to student complaints (mostly about their treatment by Heads of Schools, some of whom were treating their students like cattle) and we soon gained approval to replace the GBSM with the first modern BMus programme in a UK conservatoire (everyone else followed us within a few years). The BMus has since flourished.

'The teaching in 1990 was very old-fashioned, and very "school-centred" – the students were effectively the property of their Heads of School, and came to lectures only when they were not required for some school activity. I quickly stopped that, developing the culture of an integrated course while respecting the special demands of performance, rehearsal, opera, etc. The BMus course was designed around the idea of blocked days, so that Heads of Schools could, if they liked, timetable an event across a whole day. "Schools weeks" were also introduced. However, when George Caird arrived he re-established the principle of the all-mighty Head of School, but was obliged to promote academic studies through pressure from the students themselves and the vice-chancellor. Postgraduate work was only informal (no certification for attendance and no exams) until I started the MA in 1994, which again quickly took off. The BMus,

MA and research degrees have all had a demonstrably positive effect on the Conservatoire.'

David Saint, who had begun life as a visiting tutor in organ and paperwork at the Birmingham School of Music over thirty years earlier, took over as Acting Principal on Caird's departure in 2010. For some arcane reason within the labyrinth of BCU politics and finances he was not actually confirmed as Principal for several years, but his service during the entire period of his tenure was typical of his generosity of spirit, his warmth of personality and his constant concern for the interests of the students. During all of this time he was serving as the highly successful Director of Music at Birmingham's Catholic St Chad's Cathedral.

These are his reminiscences, his first impressions of a dynamic institution mirrored in the circumstances in which he was to leave, nearly forty years later.

'My first impression was in 1978 somewhat influenced by the route to the Birmingham School of Music's front door – through a deserted building site! Although unprepossessing, it nevertheless suggested to me a building and institution on the brink of development and expansion.

'The first members of staff I met were John Bishop (who appointed me to the Organ Department),

Louis Carus and Peter James, Director of Studies. An impressive bunch! My memory tells me that there were around only 180 students back then, and of course there were no degree courses. However, the small number of students I met were of a good standard and John Bishop and George Miles were undoubtedly a significant draw for organists.

'I began with just a few hours a week of organ and theory teaching. My role grew incrementally, with changes every two or three years. The main jobs were Assistant Course Director, Course Director, Head of Undergraduate Studies, Associate Dean, Vice-Principal and, for the last five years, Principal.

'However able I may or may not have been, I was certainly lucky and repeatedly found myself in the right place at the right time. I think most people would have had to move across several institutions to achieve a similar series of roles – something I would have been reluctant to do.'

David Saint lists some of the significant changes he has witnessed during his thirty-eight years on the staff of Birmingham Conservatoire.

'One, the opening of the Adrian Boult Hall – helped us walk tall!

'Two, the introduction of degree awards – we led the way here and, on balance, there is a better chance of our graduates being well-rounded musicians.

'Three, the growth of the international student body – brings a new dimension to the overall student experience.

'Four, the development of research – having in-house, world-leading expertise has brought so many new opportunities for staff and students.

'From being perceived as something of a poor relation in the conservatoire world, I would say that our reputation is finally catching up with what is in fact the reality. We're increasingly a destination of first choice, and at this end of my career I can say with certainty that our offer to students is second to none. Birmingham has a world-class music scene and a world-class Conservatoire!'

Peter Johnson similarly feels that the standing of the Conservatoire at the time of his retirement was 'very high. In research, beating the Royal Academy of Music, and level with the Royal College of Music and the Royal Northern College of Music . . . conservatoires are now about much more than creating orchestra fodder. In jazz we are probably leaders in the UK, and in composition among the leaders.'

At last today Birmingham Conservatoire is comfortably ensconced as a scion of Birmingham City University, with an administration that recognises and indeed embraces the enthusiasm of the current Principal, Julian Lloyd Webber.

His Royal Highness Prince Edward, Earl of Wessex, enjoys a concert in the old building's Recital Hall in the company of David Roberts, Dean of the Faculty of Arts, Media and Design at Birmingham City University, and Julian Lloyd Webber, Principal of Birmingham Conservatoire. The Earl of Wessex has for many years been Patron of the City of Birmingham Symphony Orchestra, and in 2016 he also graciously agreed to become Patron of Birmingham Conservatoire.

Lloyd Webber was appointed as Principal of Birmingham Conservatoire in the summer of 2015, at a time when his own career as a performer had reached a crossroads. Half a century of cello-playing had led to a repetitive strain injury in the area between his neck and shoulder, and his last few performances had been given in great pain, leading him to announce his retirement from the concert platform.

But he was not leaving his life as a professional musician behind, as he now began pursuing a career as a conductor, obtaining readings from orchestras refreshing in their directness. As part of the City of Sounds Festival, which marked the closure of the Adrian Boult Hall in the Paradise Circus building prior to its demolition, Lloyd Webber conducted the City of Birmingham Symphony Orchestra in Haydn's C major Cello Concerto, with orchestra principal and Conservatoire tutor Eduardo Vassallo as soloist. He has also conducted successful concerts with the Stratford-based Orchestra of the Swan, and has recorded a CD of English music.

So the advertising of a Principal's vacancy could not have come at a more apposite time. Julian Lloyd Webber had been used to a life jetting around the world from his metropolitan London base, but he came to be interested in a move to the city that London continues to regard (I suspect out of jealousy) as a poor relation.

'It was the promise of the new Conservatoire that attracted me. David Roberts, Dean of the Faculty of Arts, Media and Design, showed me round the campus site and the potential of cross-collaborations was immediately apparent. We are in a position to be able develop in many ways – as an example, merging with the School of Acting opens up possibilities for a Musical Theatre course, and so on.

'Artistically the place seemed to be on a high and I was very impressed with the Heads of Departments. They are all ambitious – more for the Conservatoire than themselves. I am trying hard to keep some of them as they keep being offered other jobs!'

For so many decades the staff members were largely home grown, but now the roster boasts many illustrious international names. 'There is a special feeling about the city – perhaps that it's on the verge of something very big and people want to stay to be part of it,' Julian says.

There is also more of a family atmosphere at the major cultural organisations. They like to work together – it's not so cut-throat as in London. This is especially true at the Conservatoire where students really do help each other to develop. Regarding student intake – this will be dictated by the importance different countries attach to introducing children to music. In the Far East children learning to play an instrument is 'the norm'. In many Western countries this can longer be said to be the case.

Julian Lloyd Webber is passionate about the need for every child to have access to music education, and despairs at the atmosphere of philistinism that prevails among this country's political elite, which seems sanguine about it being only children from families that can afford it who can benefit from instrumental tuition.

Playing a musical instrument brings self-confidence, self-esteem, a sense of achievement, and performing with others – whether in an orchestra, or in a chamber ensemble, or as a duo – brings discipline, awareness, responsibility and empathy. And all these desiderata are heightened by the Conservatoire experience.

There have always been questions about how an institution such as the Conservatoire should be funded. Specialist music education is expensive, and ways must be found of filling the gap between what most students pay and what it costs to teach them. How far should students in other subjects be expected to foot the bill? What is the price of excellence?

Those are live questions. But you have only to look at the new building and experience its capabilities to gauge the level of support Birmingham Conservatoire has received in recent years.

'Birmingham Conservatoire has the potential to be the best in the world. I really believe that, as its facilities will be unparalleled. We have already shown we can attract the best teachers and students – but we *must* be allowed to "fly",' Lloyd Webber concludes. There has never been more of an atmosphere of outreach and aspiration, and never before has the Conservatoire been such a flagship of international excellence.

RECOLLECTIONS

Clorinda Smith

1950s

I liked the Midland Institute, the grandeur of the main staircase, and I liked the large, cold room heated by a small two-bar electric fire where I had my piano lessons with Lilian Niblette. I liked *her*, talking with a cigarette in her mouth, coughing, black eyes twinkling, talking about Schumann as though she knew him. The romance of it all!

I had viola lessons with Lena Wood, another smoking, choking music teacher, fag in mouth, ash all over her instrument. I liked her too, in spite of her suggesting, at the end of the first year, that I might think about changing instruments. She was right – the viola just wasn't me. Lena, as we were allowed to call her, said that our student orchestra was short of a bassoon, and she happened to know that the BSM had an instrument I could borrow.

So I started lessons with 'Ronnie' Vaughan Allen. He was great fun, if a little flirty, although he never stepped over the line. I absolutely loved the bassoon. Ronnie was with the CBSO, as was James, or Jimmy, Beaumont, the percussionist who taught me to paradiddle, and how to tune the kettle drums, never rushing it, between

'In exasperation at our ruining a masterpiece, he often hissed at us while we played in orchestra, "Butchers! Murderers!"'

movements. A lot of the instrument teachers were from the CBSO. My brother had trumpet lessons with Ken Clewlow, who became a great friend of mine.

I had Aural Training with George Miles, and Theory with Clarence Raybould who conducted our orchestra. He was also a composer who knew Granville Bantock and Sibelius. I remember that fellow student Gill Kaye, cellist, and I planned to go to Finland to meet our hero. 'Clarry' (not to his face) said he would write a letter of introduction for us to take. Then Sibelius died!

Dr Raybould, as I think we normally addressed him, taught me very little (although I was in need of remedial help), but we got on very well, sipping sherry through the lesson, he talking of his experiences. In exasperation at our ruining a masterpiece, he often hissed at us while we played in orchestra, 'Butchers! Murderers!'

I was at the School of Music from 1954 to 1957. The third year I continued having lessons and many of us joined the brand new Midland Youth Orchestra, trained and conducted by Blyth Major. By this time our Principal was the rather dashing Sir Steuart Wilson. We didn't know then of his campaign against homosexuals in the music business. I liked Sir 'Stewpot' (his inevitable nickname).

There were 'celebrity' musicians who visited the BSM, usually to give a concert or a talk. Joseph Cooper came and played Schumann, and talked about him. Archie Camden, the bassoonist, also did an illustrated talk, which was particularly interesting for me. One year, the Master of the Queen's Music, Sir Arthur Bliss joined us for our Christmas lunch. There were fortnightly 'in-house' concerts where various students, including the part-timers who had evening lessons, played for fellow students, friends and families. And something called, mysteriously to me, the Conversazione. I think this happened once a year and perhaps it included meetings to discuss the arts, but for me it was dressing-up time and dancing in the Town Hall. Looking back, and thinking of today's youthful gatherings, we were very well behaved. I don't remember anyone ever getting really drunk, or behaving badly.

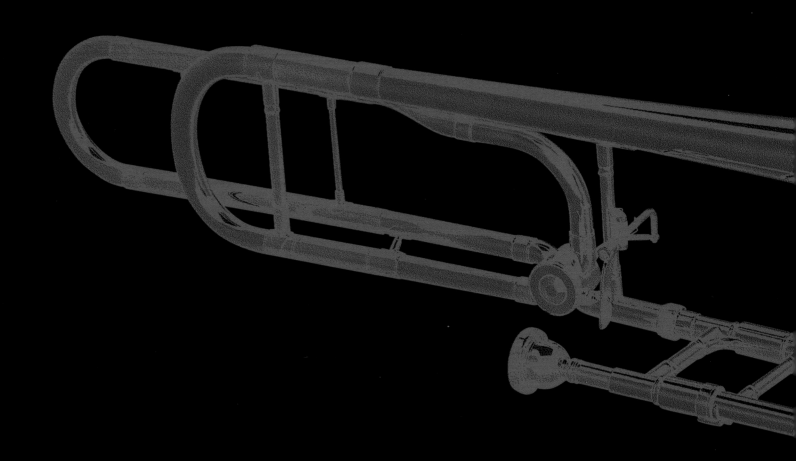

2 A SEARCH FOR A HOME

When the Birmingham School of Music emerged blinking into the world and found its feet as an entity within the Birmingham and Midland Institute a century and a half ago it was housed in an imposing, protective building within a cultural triangle that had Birmingham Town Hall and the Central Library at its other corners.

The exterior breathed solidity; the interior was gradually modified over the decades to provide adequate teaching, practice, performance and administrative facilities, and everything seemed set for a cosy, safe and settled future.

Things were stirring beyond the BMI's four walls, however. The need to reconstruct Birmingham city centre after heavy bombing during the Second World War led to plans to create an inner ring road, a highway whose route would in fact cut right through the BMI and the Central Library. No one would dare touch the Town Hall, so the drawings tended towards the option of demolishing the buildings opposite.

As the planning progressed, so the need to identify premises for the relocation of the BMI intensified. The School of Music was certainly the largest and busiest component of the organisation, and its accommodation would be a major factor in the choice of a new venue.

But a counterpoint to all this was the constant undercurrent of friction that had grown and festered over the decades between the BMI Council and the School of Music itself, which had felt fettered by the administrative procedures of the Institute. In the event this enforced eviction from Paradise Street brought the issue to a head, and the separation duly happened, with the BMI moving to elegant premises in Margaret Street and the School of Music moving to semi-derelict premises in Dale End, on the edge of the city centre.

The BMI's Margaret Street residence made it a next-door neighbour of the Birmingham School of Art, while the School of Music had to rub along with various rundown establishments at the end of a road that led, basically, nowhere. Its home was now in what had once been an impressive terracotta building housing the Young Men's Christian Association, and had later become the administrative headquarters of the Midlands Electricity Board. These premises had been half-demolished but still boasted an impressive entrance hall and marble staircase.

This was the base for the School of Music during the next seven years, until the reshaping of Paradise Circus was complete and a new home for the BSM was built above the Fletchers Walk shopping subway, ironically on virtually the selfsame spot where the old

The crunchers assailed the Adrian Boult Hall in June 2016, immediately after the fare-well performance of the Verdi Requiem, and a recording for CD release of John Joubert's South of the Line, performed by Conservatoire forces under Paul Spicer.

Conservatoire Principal Julian Lloyd Webber shows Mirga Gražinytė-Tyla, newly appointed music director of the CBSO, around the developing Conservatoire building on Eastside.

Birmingham and Midland Institute had stood. The building was opened by Queen Elizabeth The Queen Mother in 1973.

These new premises were already too small to be fit for purpose: the entrance was unprepossessing, the administrative facilities were cramped, and there was no provision for large-scale concert performance. For many years the BSM Symphony Orchestra and choruses were forced to give concerts in the restricted area of the Recital Hall, with barely space for any kind of sizeable audience.

The problem of extending the building to accommodate an adequate concert hall exercised the powers-that-were for several years. One solution favoured for a while by the City of Birmingham Education Department (the body then responsible for the administration of the School of Music under the aegis of the City of Birmingham Polytechnic) was the idea of combining a concert hall with a gymnasium for the use of the Birmingham Athletic Institute, which also came under the Education Department's umbrella – pragmatism gone mad.

Fortunately, wise counsels prevailed, and in 1986 the Adrian Boult Hall was opened by the Duchess of Gloucester in an extension at the Town Hall end of the original building. Considerable thought had gone

THE FIDDLE AND BONE

In the concluding years of the last century, two players in the City of Birmingham Symphony Orchestra – first violinist Mark Robinson and trombonist Danny Longstaff – took over a derelict early nineteenth-century canalside building at the bottom of Sheepcote Street, just off Birmingham's Broad Street, and turned it into a pub named the Fiddle and Bone.

The venue became famous for its real ale, its decent pub meals, and above all for its daily offerings of live music in all kinds of genres, encompassing folk, jazz, rock and classical. Many of the performers were Birmingham Conservatoire students, learning their trade in a sympathetic environment.

Probably one of the most surreal events ever emanating from the establishment occurred during one of the Fiddle and Bone's annual 1827 festivals, celebrating the year of the opening of the adjacent canal, the founding of their main brewery, and marking the death of Beethoven with bizarre performances of all nine symphonies using a variety of instrumental line-ups, with a chorus for the Ninth drawn from whomever could be parted from their pints.

It was a public melting-pot in which Conservatoire students mixed with CBSO players and indeed conductors, as well as music critics. And many of the students found pint-pulling jobs there, too. Others found stewarding jobs at Symphony Hall, where they were able to rub shoulders with the greatest names in the international world of music.

Sadly, neighbours complained about the noise, and prevailed on councillors to get the premises closed.

into the naming of the facility, and in the event this particular nomenclature was chosen in honour of a conductor who had been closely associated with the City of Birmingham Orchestra (renamed the City of Birmingham Symphony Orchestra in 1948) since soon after its founding in 1920 and with the Birmingham Festival Choral Society.

Kevin Thompson says:

'The Birmingham city fathers promised Adrian Boult a new concert hall as early as the 1920s. Here he has one.

'And if you mention the Adrian Boult Hall anywhere around the world, people immediately associate it with Birmingham Conservatoire.'

Former Chief Executive of the City of Birmingham Tom Caulcott remembers the part he played in the creation of the Adrian Boult Hall:

'I arrived in Birmingham as Chief Executive of the City in early 1982. Although in no way an executant, I have always been interested in music so it was quite natural that as well as signing up for a season ticket at the CBSO I got in touch with what was then the Birmingham School of Music, and became friends with Louis Carus, the then Head of School.

'1982 still saw the previous economic down-turn but the government were prepared to give new grants for public-sector capital investment. I persuaded

the City to apply and we had a major project of completing the Paradise Circus development which, after the library had been built, had stopped in its tracks, involving the completion of the BSM with the building of the Adrian Boult Hall.

'Symphony Hall at that stage was no more than a gleam in my eye. So it was in the ABH that the CBSO held their rehearsals and had their offices in the BSM building. Because this was the completion of an earlier project, the City was under contract to use the previous developer's architect. So there was no question of a new acoustician for the ABH, as later there would be for Symphony Hall.

'I well remember when we tried out the acoustics of the new ABH with Simon Rattle and the CBSO playing Berlioz!'

David Saint, who'd been on the Conservatoire staff since 1978, remembered how everyone had felt when the idea of creating a comfortable, purpose-built concert hall was first mooted:

'The area was a wasteland, with access to the School of Music through a pair of double doors into a cramped foyer. So we were very excited when it was transformed into one of the finest conservatoire concert halls of its time.'

'The Adrian Boult Hall developed into a venue for the wider city,' reminisced George Caird.

'Mondays were always Simon Rattle days, when he rehearsed the CBSO. There was amazing music-making, with excitement all around the house, and students queuing for coffee behind Simon and the CBSO Chief Executive Officer Ed Smith.

'Other organisations used the hall, and we were a natural hub for activity. And then there was the annual Music for Youth festival, with hundreds of young people performing here!'

Further modifications were carried out to the building, meanwhile, including the opening up of an area above the Fletchers Walk shops and restaurants, known as 'The Void'. This provided additional practice rooms, and the opportunity to create what was ambitiously described as the New Lecture Theatre. In the event this last enterprise proved a huge disappointment to anyone who was envisaging a tiered room in which students looked down onto the teaching area, much in the manner of Rembrandt's *The Anatomy Lesson*; all that transpired was a largish hall totally lacking in atmosphere, and bisected by a huge pillar, which interfered with sightlines between the lecturer and the class of students.

Year by year every summer saw redecorations, recarpeting and various other modifications. Obviously the University was investing optimistically in the premises of its Conservatoire. The most spectacular

'The area was a wasteland, with access to the School of Music through a pair of double doors into a cramped foyer.'

This computer-generated image shows the environment of the new Conservatoire to be vastly different from that of its land-locked predecessor.

refurbishment was the refitting of the Recital Hall, improving its acoustic capabilities, changing its seating and making a feature of its organ. Significantly, no organ had ever been installed in the Adrian Boult Hall, though various good intentions had been expressed.

Alarm bells about an enforced removal were once again ringing, rendering all this expensive tinkering analogous to the repositioning of the deckchairs on the *Titanic*. Birmingham City Council had grand plans to transform Paradise Circus, demolishing Fletchers Walk and the rather tacky Paradise Forum, evicting traders from both locations; demolishing the controversial Central Library (described by one architectural expert as a 'carbuncle on the face of a dear friend'), and demolishing the entire Conservatoire. The land thus acquired would be sold off for the creation of high-rise office and hotel developments.

Various re-sitings had been in the frame over the years, including the depressingly vacant Palladian-style Birmingham Municipal Bank building on Broad Street, opposite Symphony Hall and round the corner from the CBSO Centre in Berkley Street. Then there was Louisa Ryland House (named after one of Birmingham's greatest benefactresses), right next door to the magnificent Birmingham School of Art in

Margaret Street and Edmund Street and, ironically, just around the corner from the Birmingham and Midland Institute.

But then came the lightbulb moment, and a golden opportunity for Birmingham City University (the new name for the University of Central England, the erstwhile City of Birmingham Polytechnic), which was keen to assemble all its constituent faculties from seven different locations across the city onto one campus in Eastside, a derelict area of the city beyond Moor Street Station, Digbeth and Corporation Street. Prudent Brummies had avoided the vicinity, particularly at night, but as a result of BCU's building of new homes for its various departments the area has since become vibrant, attractive and family-friendly, with plenty of enticing play areas and water features. Signing is bright and informative, and those passing through no longer feel threatened. And the obvious solution for the homeless musicians was to create a spectacular, state-of-the-art, purpose-built new home, a glamorous edifice to reflect the glittering stature of Birmingham Conservatoire in the international world of music.

New Street and Moor Street train stations are within easy walking distance, and at the heart of the BCU complex of buildings lies the still-intact Curzon Street station, the original terminus of the London

The new Conservatoire has been designed to be both user- and audience-friendly.

and Midland Railway, built in 1838 as an archway to mirror the one at the London end of the line at Euston, which finally ceased operating in 1966. There had been plans in recent years to make Curzon Street the home of the Royal College of Organists, with the Conservatoire housing its voluminous library, and the Queen indeed planted a rose in the tiny garden outside as a token of the RCO's arrival. However, various financial and legal issues militated against the move. That rose is no more.

But it is good to know that the station is still there, within a stone's throw of the remarkable new Conservatoire building, and providing a link with Mendelssohn, who arrived at Curzon Street whenever he appeared at the Birmingham Triennial Musical Festivals (including for the premiere of *Elijah*), and who indeed made an evocative pasticcio sketch of the station and its vicinity.

Initially there had been some criticism of the new Conservatoire's design by Fielden Clegg Bradley Studios as Stalinist and Brutalist. To be honest, the computer-generated concrete-like projections of the building had failed to reveal that the exterior would in fact be fetchingly clad in warm brick.

There were two important considerations involved. One was to afford the students the most perfect acoustic facilities, in practice rooms and in

'A glamorous edifice to reflect the glittering stature of Birmingham Conservatoire in the international world of music.'

Computer-generated images
showing the planned new studios,
for practice and recording.

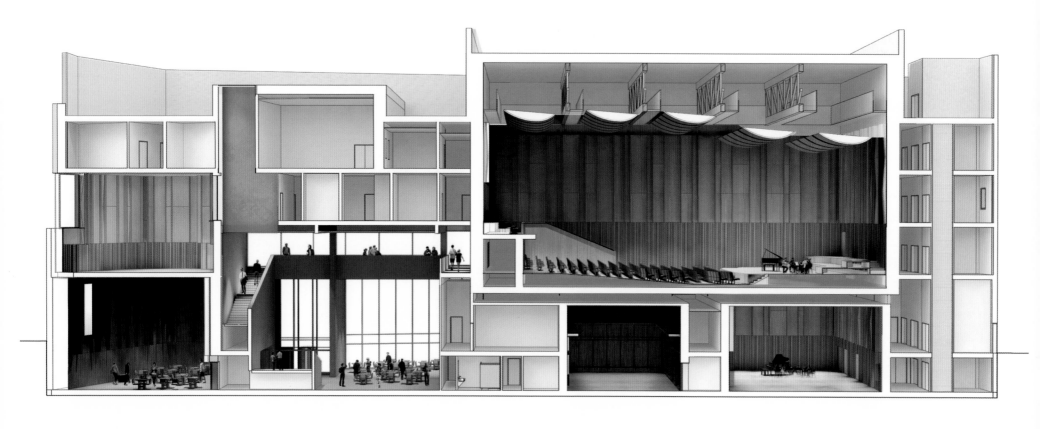

Architect's impression of the cross-section interior of the new building.

OPPOSITE Computer-generated image showing students using the new available space, both as performers and audience.

CLOSING-TIME AT THE ABH

Closing time at the Adrian Boult Hall was an event no one present will easily forget, not least the hundreds of instrumentalists and choristers, and conductor Barry Wordsworth, eleventh-hour hero of the evening on 26 June 2016.

This comfortable concert hall within Birmingham Conservatoire was in existence for only thirty years, during which time many of the world's greatest performers and composers have graced its stage. A gala presentation of the Verdi *Requiem* was its last-ever public event.

And it was so fitting that this account should be conducted by Wordsworth, a student of Sir Adrian, and who drew from these Conservatoire students and colleagues a performance brimming with vigour, depth of tone, subtlety, colour, detail, dynamic range, flexibility, security of pitch and tempo, and a hugely touching sincerity.

Yet until forty-eight hours beforehand he had thought he would be appearing only for a pre-concert interview reminiscing about Boult – and what a fascinating session that turned out to be. But then the announced conductor withdrew, and Wordsworth, who was in France at the time, received the call.

One would never have realised the backstage drama behind this reading. Wordsworth brought such calm, clear authority to proceedings, and guided with understated wisdom a remarkably excellent solo quartet – soprano Caroline Modiba, mezzo Victoria Simmonds, tenor David Butt Philip, bass Barnaby Rea – through their demanding, often *Aida*-like contributions.

Particular orchestral highlights were the confidence of the cellos at the cruelly exposed opening to the *Offertorio*, and the sturdy panache of the brass (the rare cimbasso rasping away) in the *Dies irae*.

Upper-gallery trumpets had also figured in a neat little opener, *Carrier*, by Belgian post-grad student Maya Verlaak, a three-minute fanfare based on acronyms of ACBH, as blazing as anything by Janáček, and tautly delivered under Christopher Houlding.

Nobody wanted to leave at the end of this very special concert.

Julian Lloyd Webber conducts the CBSO and its principal cellist Eduardo Vassallo in a Haydn Cello Concerto, as part of a series of concerts leading up to the closure of the Adrian Boult Hall.

Barry Wordsworth, who came to the rescue at the eleventh hour to conduct a searing Verdi Requiem at the Adrian Boult Hall closing concert, discusses his studies with Sir Adrian in a pre-concert interview with the author.

OPPOSITE Sir James and Lady Jeanne Galway were in residence at Birmingham Conservatoire during the final term of the Adrian Boult's Hall existence. They continue to be much-valued visitors.

performance areas. This desideratum has almost certainly been achieved. The other is to attract audiences down into what has previously been an 'iffy' area of Birmingham, making them feel safe and wanted.

An enticing factor will be the proximity of the new Conservatoire to the proposed railway station servicing HS2, though that will come into existence only long after the opening of this new building. 'The university will be the first thing you see from the train' is the idea.

This first new-build UK conservatoire since 1987 comprises five performance venues, including a public concert hall with capacity for over 450 and a full orchestra, a 150-seat recital hall, a smaller experimental music space, and organ and jazz rooms. There are also over seventy practice rooms of various sizes, all insulated from each other.

The organ studio has been particularly meticulously designed, as former Conservatoire Principal David Saint enthusiastically told me. 'A three-second reverberation has been built into the acoustic,' he said, 'and it's a sixty-seater room.'

There are some possible downsides to this cross-city relocation. Many of the Conservatoire students have traditionally boosted their finances by stewarding at Symphony Hall, just across Centenary Square from the old Conservatoire building. Another benefit is the way they have been able to rub shoulders, gaining valuable experience, with the world-class artists performing in one of the world's greatest concert halls. Perhaps the trek from Eastside, especially when purpose-built student accommodation is constructed in the learning quarter, won't be so congenial.

As well it might not be for players of the CBSO, long-time stalwarts of the Conservatoire's instrumental teaching staff, who might not relish schlepping a mile or two across the city traffic.

But the mood remains determinedly upbeat. David Saint is excited at the way acoustic science and design have advanced since the original Adrian Boult Hall was built in the 1980s and will certainly enhance the performing spaces within the new building, and the way the public is welcomed:

'I think it will be considerably better than in the old Conservatoire [building]. There will be a big open space, an interesting space, because Jennens Road, where the new building is, is higher than the slope down to Millennium Point. So there are stairs up to the Adrian Boult entrance, and down to the foyer and Recital Hall, jazz studio, experimental

Barry Wordsworth conducts his one and only rehearsal of the Verdi Requiem. The soloists, a mix of amateur and professional, are perched aloft in a side-gallery.

The full performing forces of the Verdi Requiem in rehearsal with Barry Wordsworth conducting.

music space, coffee bars – and there's a crush bar in there somewhere!'

Continuity with the past has not been neglected. Tom Caulcott explains:

'One of the results of the Education Department's limited funding of the Conservatoire was that much depended on voluntary activity. Before the formal opening of ABH in 1986 and in celebration of the centenary of the BSM, the BSM Trust Fund was established. This was run by Pamela Hobson and Jane Allsop. The City's then General Purposes Committee nominated Jane to be the City representative. This trust fund raised over £100,000 then to help BSM students.'

The BSM Centenary Appeal Trust is still going from strength to strength and Jane continues as a trustee.

'Pamela Hobson led a drive to get every seat in the ABH individually sponsored, which she achieved. All the seats have a dedication. The Trust agreed that when the new ABH opens in the new Conservatoire building, there will be a plaque giving all the names of the original ABH seat donors.'

Whatever the discomfort felt by students and staff at the accommodation in the various homes of the Birmingham School of Music and its eventual reincarnation as Birmingham Conservatoire, the end result was always the same: total affection for the institution, the opportunities it offered and the memory-bank it built for all involved in this shrine to music-making.

RECOLLECTIONS

Richard Leigh Harris

1970s

I arrived at the BSM in September 1975. In those days, the entrance to the School of Music was nearer the old Night and Day pub and the ATV studios, right at the end of that wind tunnel of a corridor that ran underneath the college.

The first thing that you encountered was the chilly entrance foyer with its equally chilly and monosyllabic porters. Their dark Corporation uniforms contrasted rather starkly with the redness of their faces. One of them, however, was a jovial Irishman. When I attended my audition he greeted me with the immortal words, 'Follow me, I'll be right behind yer!' and led the way upstairs.

The one thing I will never forget during my first week was that feeling of anticipation heightened by nervousness and, specifically, of walking down one of the corridors and hearing what sounded like all these absolutely *fantastic* musicians. Acoustically speaking, the whole experience was akin to hearing all those simultaneous musics in Cage's *Musicircus!*

'The whole college was very friendly – almost like one large and convivial extended family.'

Louis Carus also began his tenure as Principal at the same time (autumn 1975) and Dr Peter James was his second in command. Peter also conducted the School of Music Chorus every Monday evening. The repertoire included the usual oratorical suspects, but also rarely heard items such as Liszt's setting of Psalm XIII. Beadily noting our attendance (or otherwise) was the formidable librarian, Susan Clegg, who would be standing at the entrance to the Recital Hall, register in hand, with all the relaxed demeanour of an SS guard.

Due to the small number of students, the whole college was very friendly – almost like one large and convivial extended family. Students in the second and third years, for example, often went out of their way to make you feel welcome and to help you in whatever ways were needed. Not that I'm implying that this doesn't happen now, incidentally.

Many of my fellow students on the Graduate course – the class of '78 – were very astute, gifted and talented, including Jean Rigby, the acclaimed alto, who started as a pianist. Often the finest singers start off as pianists, or so it seems. The old stereotypes seemed to prevail, i.e. brass players drank excessively; string players had various neuroses, etc. I never did find out what keyboard players were meant to have!

There was never any doubt, I think, vis-à-vis the calibre of the staff, both full time as well as the visiting tutors. I studied piano with Malcolm Wilson, the harpsichord with George Miles and my weekly paperwork tutor was Tony Cross.

All three made a lasting impact on me, both musically and personally. Dear old George had been an organ student of a pupil of Reger and had a very thorough, Germanic approach to issues such as fingering. Beneath the apparent crustiness and the green corduroy jacket lay a kind and very wise man. Tony was a veritable fount of wisdom on twentieth-century music and he was, quite rightly, a demanding teacher with regard to the completion of Palestrina excerpts. Fond memories include him playing through the Liszt Sonata and introducing me to the music of Hanns Eisler.

After leaving Birmingham I took the one-year PGCertEd at Reading University. From the early 1990s until the present time, I have been a Visiting Tutor in Composition at the Conservatoire. The main change I've seen, I suppose, was when composition became a bona fide choice for students' first study. Andrew Downes led a fairly small department initially, but this gradually expanded into the widely respected department that we now have with a dozen or so composition tutors, many of whom have an international reputation. The department is now under the benevolent eyes and ears of Joe Cutler and Michael Wolters. Composition teaching at this institute has, thank God, never held to one 'house' style or way of doing things. Stylistically speaking, things are very democratic and all the tutors seek to bring out the best in their students. Thank heavens for a wide-ranging pluralism!

Helen Cross (Mills)

1970s

I was one of very few students from the Birmingham area; the general draw was definitely national. Being a relatively small college, there really was a friendly, family atmosphere which made people settle in very quickly. John Bishop's Sunday afternoon sherry party for freshers, though a little old-fashioned even by 1975 standards, did help things along in those first few days, even if one or two older lads were hanging around outside to size up the (non-musical) talent!

The calibre of students and staff was higher than I had expected too. Having had very limited experience prior to starting my course there, particularly where the flute was concerned – I'd been playing for only around three years when I was accepted – I was a bit intimidated. My first year coincided with that of new Principal Louis Carus. My feeling is that the standard at the college definitely moved up and on during his time as Principal.

I came in just after several key members of the academic staff had become established and the academic and theoretical side of things was pretty good, well organised, and continued to develop during the time I was there, including the luxury of one-to-one teaching on paperwork, keyboard skills, etc. This was pre-degree, but they introduced an 'Hons' level to the GBSM course/qualification which was supposed to be equivalent to a degree.

For the number of students around then, the building felt fairly comfortable. There were the usual niggles about practice-room availability, though this probably wasn't helped by what went on in those fourth-floor practice rooms some of the time! Of course this was pre-ABH so we only had the Recital Hall, which wasn't big enough for some of the big works we performed (e.g. Britten's *War Requiem*, for instance, which we did at St Chad's, I think).

I do remember the degree validation being a big thing when it happened, and the change of name to 'Conservatoire' which seemed to be treated with derision by some members of staff at the time, but with hindsight has I think generally been regarded as a good move. With the calibre of students – and the instrumental staff – ever rising, it has been both interesting and exciting to watch the school grow in size and reputation. Of course every Principal has contributed significantly to this, each in their own way, and I think the Conservatoire has latterly become much more of a front runner, along with the Royals. The ABH was an important addition to the building, not just because of the good-sized hall that it afforded for the ever growing College but it also brought people in from outside to use the hall and come to concerts who perhaps hadn't been so aware of the Conservatoire and what it could do before then.

I suspect the beginning of the 1970s and the new building marked a point when the whole place went up a gear. We did some pretty impressive concerts along the way, including if I remember rightly one or maybe two live broadcasts on local radio, including a concerto.

There was more time for fun though – including the infamous Christmas parties. Trying to make complete fools of the staff was a big feature of them: for example, putting tubular bells in the wrong order and staff being expected to play Christmas carols on them, a string teacher being given a cello and told to play 'The Swan' with an orange on the fingerboard, and so on, all for the entertainment of the students. The other memory I have of 'fun' episodes was the Paradise Instrumental Sounds Sinfonia orchestra or something very similar – the acronym drove the title; not subtle, admittedly. Everyone involved had to play an unfamiliar instrument, the result being intentionally along the lines of the then infamous Portsmouth Sinfonia. Dick Greening, resplendent in football kit and whistle, conducted one session. Works included *Mars* from *The Planets,* and the opening of *Swan Lake,* with the oboe player being booed because he played it too well. Even the catering staff and security guys popped their heads round the door of the Recital Hall to see what was going on.

It has been heartening to see so many former students and staff attending the various reunions and how much warmth and affection there has been, both between the people attending and for the place. The pastoral-care element, which has been evident certainly since my time there, no doubt helped with this. And of course there have been quite a few marriages down the line . . .

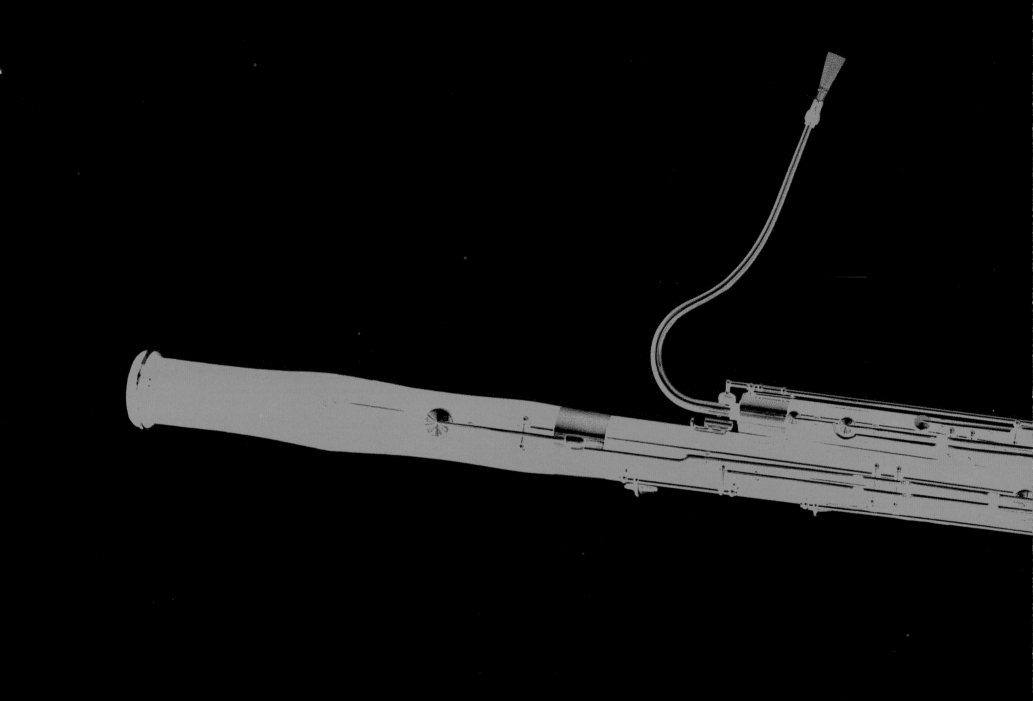

3 MAKING MUSIC

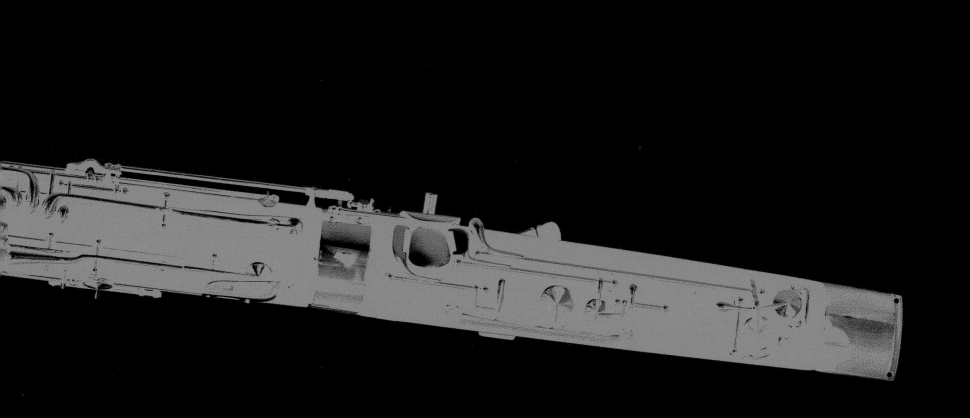

From its beginnings as a Penny Singing Class, the Birmingham School of Music expanded its focus to include tuition on wind instruments and strings – at one time the only BSM students taking external examinations were violinists – with keyboard tuition seemingly keeping a low profile. Vocal tuition was somewhat vague in its application (including the massed classes for solo singing), and the presentation of operas was very much hit and miss. We also have examples of lamentations over the dire state of the orchestra.

It was perhaps the divorce from the Birmingham and Midland Institute and the subsequent takeover by the City of Birmingham Education Department that sharpened up attitudes at the BSM, and the various departments began to evolve a more professional standing. Today the Conservatoire boasts not only departments devoted to traditional Western classical disciplines, but it also has a thriving jazz department, explores world music, and encourages an underlying thread of musical pedagogy.

One of the many flautists to train at the Conservatoire.

OPERA

lthough it was nearly half a century since the beginnings of the Birmingham School of Music before any serious operatic activity was undertaken, once launched, the BSM rapidly achieved a notable triumph in the field.

The first complete production was Gluck's *Orpheus and Eurydice*, presented in 1904, having been preceded by an abridged version of Mozart's *The Magic Flute*, fully staged and with orchestral accompaniment, the previous year. Two years later the School brought off the spectacular coup of staging the British premiere of Gluck's *Iphigenia in Aulis*, thanks to the enthusiastic advocacy of Granville Bantock, who conducted the production. Ernest Newman, who had been appointed in 1903 to teach Singing and Rudiments at the School of Music with no formal qualifications so far as this writer can trace – how can anyone presume to teach singing with no experience of the physical resources required? Black mark to the BSM – and who had published a book on Gluck, wrote the programme notes. He left in 1905 to become music critic of the *Manchester Guardian*, and was replaced by Rutland Boughton as teacher of Rudiments.

Newman subsequently returned to Birmingham in 1906, serving as music critic of the *Birmingham Daily Post* before moving to London in 1919 to become critic on the *Observer*, going on to *The Sunday Times* the

following year. He was also renowned as one of the country's greatest authorities on the life and works of Richard Wagner.

Meanwhile the Birmingham School of Music continued its pursuit of operatic activities. Unfortunately there had not been a sufficient pool of students to supply a full chorus for *Iphigenia in Aulis* – the numbers had been made up with members of the Birmingham Festival Choral Society – and when the next biennial production for 1908 came under consideration the same problem reared its head.

The success of the 1906 production had attracted the recruitment of twenty-three new students into the opera class, but Granville Bantock had to admit that as there were 'not at present any students in the School of Music capable of taking the principal parts in an opera, it has proved impossible to arrange for a public performance this year'. However, the BSM's apparent infatuation with Gluck rode over everything, and a year later, in 1909, two performances were given of his *Iphigenia in Tauris*. A production of Cornelius's *The Barber of Baghdad* was put into rehearsal as the next presentation, but there is no record of any actual performance.

Within half a decade the Birmingham School of Music had established its opera school as a vehicle for the exploration of rarely performed works, many of

Birmingham Conservatoire has always had a strong tradition of operatic production.

OPPOSITE *The climactic finale of Poulenc's* Dialogues des Carmélites, *as the sisters approach the guillotine two by two, singing 'Salve Regina'.*

RIGHT *A performance of* Suor Angelica, *the central opera in Puccini's* Il trittico.

which were destined never to become fixtures in the established repertoire of the British operatic stage, but which the BSM rightly felt part of its remit to present.

Over-subscription and easy entry to the opera class meant that casting was frequently compromised by those who had been awarded parts but who subsequently attended rehearsals intermittently. Mozart presentations during the 1930s suffered, and incurred financial losses, and Allen Blackall, Bantock's successor as Principal, set about shaking up the way the opera class was run.

Pragmatism was to prevail, with works chosen that would not stretch the School's resources, and that, presented on a small stage, would require the minimum of elaborate costumes and changes of scenery. Casting, plus the appointment of understudies, would give preference to loyal members of the class, who would need to sign a written agreement guaranteeing regular attendance and the obligation to be note- and word-perfect by the start of the rehearsal period. A severe caveat was that appearance in one production was no guarantee of appearance in the next, for which a renewed application would have to be submitted.

Whether by accident or design, the first few operas presented as a result of Blackall's directive were mainly those composed by past and present members of the BSM staff: Rutland Boughton's *Bethlehem* had incurred a financial loss, reduced by a successful production of Bantock's *The Seal Woman* in April 1936. Christopher Edmunds (a future Principal of the Birmingham School of Music) had a double-bill of his operas performed: *The Blue Harlequin* and the unfortunately titled *The Fatal Rubber*. But a projected performance of a mainstream opera, Mozart's *The Abduction from the Seraglio*, with a two-piano accompaniment, had to be abandoned as gathering war clouds were diminishing enrolment in the School.

After the Second World War the Birmingham School of Music gradually found its feet again, and operatic activities grew to become a major feature in its annual calendar, though an actual Opera Class was proving difficult to sustain, with few students showing a committed interest.

By the 1960s its list of productions had included Weber's *Der Freischütz* (1948); Tchaikovsky's *Eugene Onegin* (1950), with an improvised two-piano accompaniment, the orchestral parts having been delayed in their return from Australia – were these the only orchestral parts in the world?; Mozart's *The Marriage of Figaro* (1960), and Holst's *Sāvitri* and Puccini's *Gianni Schicchi* (1961).

STELLAR ALUMNI

Recent graduates from the School of Vocal and Operatic Studies, such as the baritone Rhydian Roberts and the soprano Laura Mvula, have made a huge impact on the show-business world.

Mvula graduated in composition, but rapidly made her name as a gospel-influenced singer, her first album, *Sing to the Moon*, reaching number 9 in the charts on its release in 2013. More recently she has returned to composition, writing the score for the Royal Shakespeare Company's production of Shakespeare's *Antony and Cleopatra* in spring 2017.

Another alumna who is making her way steadily in the realm of more serious opera is the soprano Abigail Kelly, and among her predecessors attaining huge success are the mezzo-soprano Jean Rigby, sopranos Susannah Glanville and Samantha Hay and, going back half a century, the soprano Margaret Curphey, who featured in one of the greatest triumphs ever to occur on an operatic stage in England.

Margaret sang Eva in the legendary English-language production of Wagner's *The Mastersingers* at London's Sadler's Wells Theatre in 1968, singing alongside Norman Bailey as Hans Sachs and Alberto Remedios as Walther, under the wise, measured baton of the great Reginald Goodall.

Laura Mvula has released two albums which have flown high in the charts.

A scene from the Conservatoire's Opera Triple Bill at the Crescent Theatre, showcasing performances of Vaughan Williams's Riders To The Sea, Holst's Sāvitri and Ravel's L'enfant et les sortilèges.

These last two shows were produced by the experienced duo of David Franklin, a highly regarded bass singer with performances at Glyndebourne figuring in his impressive CV, as director and Allan Bixter as conductor. Bixter's further appearances on the BSM operatic podium included Mozart's *Così fan tutte* (1964), Puccini's *Il tabarro* and the English premiere of Menotti's *The Old Maid and the Thief* (1965), Mozart's *Don Giovanni* (1966) and then many of the repertoire's staple operas.

With the arrival of Keith Darlington as Head of the BSM Vocal Department operatic productions became regular events, and standard repertoire became as much a feature as the exploration of lesser-known works. Britten operas were presented: *Albert Herring* in 1972 at the Midlands Arts Centre (and again in 1986), *A Midsummer Night's Dream* in 1974 at the Crescent Theatre, only fourteen years since its premiere. This latter production was given in association with Birmingham Polytechnic's Department of Three-Dimensional Design (Theatre Design), and the Departments of Visual Communication and Fashion and Textiles.

There were also touring productions, such as Handel's *Alcina*, performed in Bath's Pump Room in 1985, and welcome additions to the opera production fund came from appearances by the BSM Opera Chorus in Raymond Gubbay Gala Nights at the Royal Albert Hall in London.

Keith Darlington was succeeded on his retirement in 1994 by Julian Pike, a professional singer with many contacts in the operatic world. A notable factor in his career was having sung in no fewer than three instalments (*Montag, Dienstag* and *Donnerstag*) of the week-long opera *Licht* by Karlheinz Stockhausen. Under Pike's tenure conductors from outside were invited to conduct major operatic productions. These included Fraser Goulding and Stephen Barlow, the appearance of whose wife, the actress Joanna Lumley, at performances always caused a frisson.

By now the operas were reaching out into the furthest corners of the repertoire. Kurt Weill's *Street Scene* was vibrantly given at the Crescent Theatre, and a production of Poulenc's harrowing *Dialogues des Carmélites* was perhaps the most estimable presentation in the Opera School's history in over a century since that Gluck *Iphigenia in Aulis* premiere in 1906.

The merger announced early in 2017 between Birmingham Conservatoire and the Birmingham School of Acting, bringing them together into a single faculty of Birmingham City University, will facilitate further exploration and experimentation in stage performance, with the new building providing accommodating rehearsal space.

'Although it was nearly half a century since the beginnings of the Birmingham School of Music before any serious operatic activity was undertaken, once launched, the BSM rapidly achieved a notable triumph in the field.'

A scene from Ava's Wedding, an opera written by composition tutor Michael Wolters and performed at Birmingham's Crescent Theatre.

L'Enfant et les sortilèges, *an opera with music by Ravel to a libretto written by Colette, being performed at the Crescent Theatre.*

Scenes from a performance of Sāvitri by Gustav Holst, featuring Caroline Modiba as one of the soloists (left).

An annual highlight of the Conservatoire's Christmas programme includes the popular Opera Scenes feature.

Students from the vocal and operatic departments present favourite scenes from a variety of well-loved operas at the Recital Hall.

BELOW Another scene from Gianni Schicchi, *the concluding part of the trilogy.*

OPPOSITE *A production of* Gianni Schicchi, *a comic opera and part of Puccini's* Il trittico, *presented at the Crescent Theatre.*

Further examples of performances from the annual Opera Scenes; students at the Conservatoire have the opportunity to perform in a wide range of recitals and venues. Many students go on to achieve great success, including Rhydian Roberts (above and left), who went on to perform on The X Factor in 2007 and has since become a popular classical crossover artist.

'Within half a decade the Birmingham School of Music had established its opera school as a vehicle for the exploration of rarely performed works.'

Scenes from Ava's Wedding by Michael Wolters, written in 2015 with a libretto by Alexandra Taylor.

Ava's Wedding uses music
from five centuries of English
tradition, allowing students to
explore different techniques
while performing.

KEYBOARD DEPARTMENT

Although there was a brief period when the only students being presented for examination were violinists, the Keyboard Department has always been a prominent element within the Birmingham School of Music/Conservatoire.

Keyboard work in the institution has never been merely centred on aspiring performers, but has also catered for the needs of those who would be going on to careers in teaching and would therefore need facility in accompanying. Keyboard skills became a compulsory part of the syllabus for first-year students, a requirement that found me, having long since hung up my piano-playing fingers, giving weekly lessons to a young man who has now become the Head of Organ Studies at Birmingham Conservatoire – Henry Fairs, a performer of international repute, and one who bears me no grudge after my fifteen-minute sessions coaching him in figured bass.

Organ studies in this institution have always been something of a peripatetic activity since the move from the Birmingham and Midland Institute building on Paradise Street. Local churches such as the elegant Georgian St Paul's at the heart of Birmingham's Jewellery Quarter were brought into use, and where the much respected George Miles, who was also a harpsichord tutor, held his classes. There was also the

Catholic St Chad's Cathedral, still a Conservatoire performing venue today, where David Saint (Julian Lloyd Webber's predecessor as Conservatoire Principal) is organist and choirmaster, and the Anglican St Philip's Cathedral, with Conservatoire connections including David Bruce-Payne and Marcus Huxley.

The Conservatoire benefited from the acquisition of the chamber organ owned by the late Susi Jeans up in Scotland, but it could never boast a mighty instrument with several manuals, a huge array of stops, all linked to a full pedal board, and a permanent fixture on the premises.

Pianos were far more easy to accommodate, and for a while the Conservatoire enjoyed a friendly relationship with Yamaha instruments. By the time of the departure from Paradise Circus the Conservatoire was in possession of several concert-standard Steinway grands as well as dozens of excellent instruments from other makers. The staff at this time included Katherine Lam, David Quigley and Di Xiao, who themselves had all passed through the Conservatoire's portals as students, as well as tutors such as Head of Piano John Thwaites, Philip Martin and Mark Bebbington. The department also benefited from the advice of the great international pianist Peter

Conservatoire Vice-President Peter Donohoe conducts a masterclass.

Donohoe, Vice-President of the Conservatoire. Ironically, much of the piano tuition was carried out during the final crumbling year of the Paradise Circus building within the Birmingham and Midland Institute, just across Chamberlain Square. Like a naughty child or prodigal son, people might say, the Conservatoire had at last come home to its parents.

Piano and organ are the obvious instruments that spring to mind for conservatoire keyboard study, but it's an easy leap to include harpsichord, spinet, clavichord and fortepiano, tuition in all of which is thriving at the Conservatoire. Much of the success of the interest in early keyboards can be attributed to the harpsichordist Martin Perkins, himself a Conservatoire alumnus, director of a period-instrument band (the Musical and Amicable Society), and nowadays curator of an impressive collection of historical instruments from all families. The serpents are particularly impressive.

Halfway through the Conservatoire's final year in Paradise Circus the Keyboard Department mounted an all-night extravaganza in the adjacent Birmingham Town Hall, emulating the all-night jazz sessions held in that historic building over half a century earlier.

Students, staff and visiting stars, including the actor Simon Callow, narrating Richard Strauss's

Piano practice in the old Adrian Boult Hall.

SVIATOSLAV RICHTER

The great Russian pianist Sviatoslav Richter was famous for playing with the printed music on the stand above the keyboard, illuminated by a single lamp, which imparted a slightly phosphorescent glow to his features in an otherwise darkened auditorium.

On his only visit to Symphony Hall he was offered the services as page-turner of the Conservatoire's best pianist at the time. He rejected that page-turner, who happened to be a woman. Richter was a notorious misogynist.

melodrama *Enoch Arden*, all made their contributions, and pianos, harpsichords, and even the magnificent organ, its installation supervised by Mendelssohn 180 years earlier, came into play during this celebration.

As an undergraduate in the Music Department of Birmingham University in salubrious Edgbaston during the 1960s, I was required to take weekly tuition in my instrument (piano) at the Birmingham School of Music. I found my delicate way to its rather decrepit home in Dale End, on the furthest edge of the city centre, and was rewarded with the most inspiring teaching from the unfortunate lady assigned to me, Janice Williams.

Janice was more than just a clock-watching teacher. She held tea parties for all her brood: the student whose lesson had just finished, the student whose lesson this was, and the student waiting to come in next. We all passed our exams. And she took a pastoral interest in all of us. My relationship with her and her lovely family – she always seemed to be pregnant – continued for several years.

It was always a thrill to leaf through the *Radio Times* and to see that Janice was giving a live recital somewhere or other. I seem to remember Prokofiev was one of her particular strengths. This was part of the 'edge' of the Keyboard Department (it may have been the same for other disciplines): hearing our tutors broadcasting on the wireless. In those days, of course, BBC regional radio was a powerful force, and gave ears to all manner of performing musicians. I was even paid a couple of quid for being a page-turner when the great organist Norman Dyson gave a live harpsichord recital from the old BBC Carpenter Road studios in 1969.

The Keyboard Department at the Conservatoire today has a decidedly cosmopolitan feel, with students enrolling from all parts of the world, and with tutors combining their teaching duties with worldwide performing careers.

A prize-winning Conservatoire student in recital.

A SELECTION OF CONDUCTORS

Reference is made elsewhere to one-time grudging enforced participation by undergraduate students in choral and orchestral concerts. Part of the problem was the fact that major events were in the past usually directed by staff members who, however worthy their teaching, were not actually inspiring conductors on the podium.

As the Birmingham School of Music/ Conservatoire gradually gained in self-belief and stature, professional conductors were engaged to rehearse and direct choirs and orchestras, of which rescue squad the following are merely a sample.

Jonathan Del Mar, son of the great conductor Norman Del Mar (who had played French horn in Sir Thomas Beecham's Royal Philharmonic Orchestra), and who himself went on to produce a new performing edition of the Beethoven symphonies, drawn from the original sources, and now in use worldwide. As a professional conductor engaged from outside he instilled confidence in the student players, on which his successors were able to build.

Andrew Mogrelia, who first conducted as an amateur with the Leamington Spa Chamber Orchestra, and who developed into a much sought-after ballet conductor, with major recordings on the Naxos label. He conducted the Birmingham Conservatoire Symphony Orchestra's first Stravinsky *Rite of Spring*, with Britten's *War Requiem* in Birmingham Town Hall another success.

John Lubbock, founder and conductor of the Orchestra of St John's Smith Square, and with many important recordings under his belt.

Lionel Friend, with a lifetime's experience in conducting opera, symphonic repertoire and contemporary music, often with the BBC. He is now Conductor Emeritus at the Conservatoire.

Edwin Roxburgh, composer and generous advocate of the music of his colleague contemporaries.

Michael Seal, long-time sub-principal second violin with the CBSO, and now associate conductor with that orchestra, as well as achieving a reputation both at home and abroad – and a Conservatoire alumnus. Among his many memorable concerts with Conservatoire forces was another visit to Britten's *War Requiem* at Birmingham Town Hall in 2011.

Daniele Rosina, alumnus of the Conservatoire, and now Director of Conducting in the Music Department at the University of Birmingham. Daniele is a resourceful 'go-to' conductor, and by cajoling the best out of his players has the gift of putting nervous young instrumentalists at their ease.

Paul Spicer conducting the Birmingham Conservatoire Chamber Choir, with whom he has made several well-reviewed CD recordings. He is also music director of the Birmingham Bach Choir, is an accomplished composer, and was for many years a classical music producer at BBC Radio 3, based at Pebble Mill.

'As the Birmingham School of Music/Conservatoire gradually gained in self-belief and stature, professional conductors were engaged to rehearse and direct choirs and orchestras.'

The Conservatoire offers many opportunities for both orchestral and choral conducting, with an accomplished team of regular tutors as well as a variety of guest conductors.

And as a one-off, the spectacular appearance of **Barry Wordsworth**, pupil of Sir Adrian Boult, Chief Conductor of the BBC Concert Orchestra, Music Director of the Brighton Philharmonic Orchestra, who stood in at fifty-five minutes past the eleventh hour to rescue the performance of the Verdi *Requiem* that closed the Adrian Boult Hall in June 2016, and which was absolutely incandescent in effect.

There have also been orchestral workshops with conductors visiting the CBSO, as well as sessions with the CBSO's music directors, Simon Rattle and Sakari Oramo, whose direction and narrative explanation of Sibelius's *Pohjola's Daughter* remains vividly in the memory.

Also vividly memorable was an evening when Simon Rattle presided over a workshop session in which the very young but rising young conductor Daniel Harding rehearsed the Birmingham Conservatoire Symphony Orchestra in Bartók's score for the ballet *The Miraculous Mandarin*. Harding was doing an excellent job, with Rattle intervening occasionally.

At one point Rattle, President of the Conservatoire, described Harding as 'this hideously talented young man'. And dozens of hideously talented young musicians smiled in agreement.

COMPOSITION AND CREATIVE STUDIES

Despite the fact that through the decades the Birmingham School of Music had boasted such eminent composers as Granville Bantock, Rutland Boughton and Christopher Edmunds among its staff, there was for a long time no timetable for the teaching of composition.

'There was no composition course for undergraduates in any of the music colleges,' Andrew Downes, who joined the BSM staff as a tutor in 1975, remembers.

'I went to the Royal College of Music, and you could do composition at postgraduate level, which I did. It wasn't considered a suitable subject for music colleges; they thought it should be done at university, which was very silly. It needs to be done at the same place as musicians, players and singers, to try things out.'

But Andrew successfully argued for the founding of a Creative Studies Department at the BSM, as he explains:

'It was lucky; it was during Peter James's time as Director of Studies, and he was a very enlightened man, compared with most of them, and he actually asked me at the time to be in charge of developing composition, so I did.

'It was during Louis Carus's Principalship, and we had to start to argue to develop composition as a second-study subject, and then gradually it became arguable that it would be suitable as a first-study subject. And I think the BSM was the first place to do undergraduate composition.'

At first Andrew was ploughing a lonely furrow by himself:

'Well, it was only me, to start with, for the first few years. And then I think I may have asked a couple of undergraduates who'd been very, very good – Richard Leigh Harris was one, and John Webb. I asked them to do a couple of hours a week to start with, and then John Mayer.

'He was an inspiring catch, and very thrilled to come, so we got him in as composer-in-residence, and that made a big difference to have him there, attracting some very, very good students. So it grew and grew and became very big.

'And I don't think it's changed very much, which I'm very pleased about. We're very lucky that they decided to appoint Joe Cutler as my successor, because he's got exactly the same approach. It should be a very open-minded centre, getting to know about all kinds of music from all over the world.'

Andrew Downes's philosophy has certainly informed the ethos of the creative side of the Conservatoire's work. There is an active exploration

The great French composer Pierre Boulez was in residence at Birmingham Conservatoire for one magical weekend. Here he coaches student Susanna Purkess in an extract from his Le Marteau sans maître.

'Birmingham Conservatoire
has attracted some of
the world's greatest names
to give masterclasses and
indeed stay in residencies.'

*A student immersed
in composition.*

THE CONSERVATOIRE'S LINK WITH SOUTH AFRICA

Conservatoire students are teaching budding young string-players in Soweto, South Africa – without leaving their Birmingham base. This marvel is allowed to happen via the medium of Skype, and Louise Lansdown, Head of Strings at the Conservatoire, explains how the connection came about.

'I grew up in Cape Town and I studied music at university in South Africa before leaving to study in the UK. I still have family and friends in South Africa and have always maintained very close connections with my home country. In 2013 I paid a short visit to the Cape Gate MIAGI Centre for Music in Soweto and was struck by the inspirational atmosphere at the centre, but also the enormous challenges they faced. I had an inspired crazy thought in April 2015 to start the ARCO (use of the bow when playing a stringed instrument) project and met with Robert Brooks and Chris Bishop in Johannesburg to discuss. From idea to actual teaching took around eight months.

'Weekly individual instrumental lessons, mentoring and string quartet coaching are delivered by a group of sixteen students and recent graduates from Birmingham Conservatoire via video conferencing systems. Regular events occurring within Birmingham Conservatoire's String Department, such as masterclasses, workshops and performances are streamed live to South Africa for the benefit of the CMCM students. Each summer, ARCO

teachers from the UK travel to South Africa for the annual festival – an immersive musical experience, building on and solidifying skills learnt throughout the year. ARCO, although supported by Birmingham City University and Birmingham Conservatoire, is an extra-curricular project that relies on substantial external funding to function. The project is entirely voluntary – none of the ARCO teachers is paid for any of the work that they do and we all work tirelessly to fundraise, to keep the project alive.

'The inaugural festival in 2016 was truly a life-changing experience for all involved: teachers, staff, students, parents and volunteers.'

At the time of writing twenty-four young people in Soweto are benefiting from this long-distance tuition. In addition to the weekly one-to-one Skype lesson, they form themselves into six string quartets, also receiving weekly chamber music coaching sessions. Regular events occurring in the Conservatoire Strings Department, such as masterclasses, workshops and performances, are live-streamed to South Africa.

The idea is for participants at both ends of the communication link to see the power of music as a tool for social cohesion and personal development first-hand between musicians in different environments, and from different cultures.

Every strand of ARCO's project is continually scrutinised, and to ensure maximum

effectiveness self-evaluation and record-making takes place after every instrumental lesson given via Skype, both by students and teachers. The Birmingham-based participants are required to consider the knowledge they have imparted and how it was conveyed so that, as well as the children in Soweto learning, the participants from Birmingham Conservatoire develop as teachers.

Dr Lansdown concludes by explaining the extra benefits the project offers to Birmingham Conservatoire students.

'Many conservatoire graduates enter into what is known as a "portfolio career" made up of freelance performing and instrumental teaching. ARCO gives students at Birmingham Conservatoire the opportunity to experience instrumental teaching first hand, prior to the commencement of their careers, under the supervision of an experienced pedagogue.

'Increasingly important skills related to modern technology – broadcasting, video editing, live streaming – and the practical aspect of distance learning are a challenge for all of us. These technological skills are also important for the freelance musician – skills which are not included in credited activities at the university.

'So far involvement in the scheme has resulted in unimaginable personal and cultural growth, informing our participants in terms of their artistic and personal futures in music.'

of world music, launched during the 1980s by the composer and performer Mark Lockett. This was responsible for an invasion of cockroaches into the Paradise Circus building's heating system, when they escaped as a venerated gamelan was being unpacked after its journey from Indonesia.

The Conservatoire's in-depth immersion in jazz has made it a focal point in that vibrant world, with Jeremy Price as its popular course leader and the vastly experienced Tony Dudley-Evans as adviser. Graduates have gone out into the commercial world fully and confidently equipped to handle all its pressures and demands.

And in terms of composition itself, Birmingham Conservatoire has attracted some of the world's greatest names to give masterclasses and indeed stay in residencies. Among them have been Jonathan Harvey, Richard Rodney Bennett, Pierre Boulez – 'That was incredible!' comments Downes, 'and we also got the very religious man, John Tavener.'

Probably the most awe-inspiring of these visiting composers was the huge – daunting to some – figure of Karlheinz Stockhausen, actually a delightful person, who spent several days in Birmingham in July 1992 preparing a performance of his *Sternklang* ('Park Music for Five Groups') in the city's Cannon Hill Park. The Conservatoire provided one of the five groups for this extraordinary piece, performed during the hours of gathering darkness and eventual moonrise. As the proceedings concluded the great man shook my hand and declared himself well pleased.

A spin-off from the work of the Composition Department at Birmingham Conservatoire has been the Thallein Ensemble, an instrumental group of flexible forces established around the same time as the *Sternklang* performance by students who had studied at summer schools in Darmstadt under Stockhausen and his colleagues, dedicated to the exploration of works contributing to the thrust of contemporary music. As memory recalls, the chronologically earliest work performed by the Thallein is Schoenberg's First Chamber Symphony, written in 1906, and their questing explorations under a variety of student and professional conductors continue to unearth riches.

Recent graduates from the Composition Department founded by Andrew Downes include Sam Bordoli, acclaimed as a composer of site-specific works (such as for the sleeper train between London and Scotland), Charlotte Bray (with a BBC Proms commission among her many works) and Laura Mvula, who, in addition to her public persona as a charismatic singer, is now moving towards composition for stage and screen.

The department has grown exponentially since its modest launch, and now boasts tutors drawn from an international spectrum, co-ordinated under the genial leadership of Joe Cutler.

CHORAL ACTIVITY

In the past what was then the Birmingham School of Music used to struggle to recruit and motivate a choir to take part in public concerts. Attendance at rehearsals was unwilling and uncooperative (undergraduates were virtually on a three-line whip), and performances were perfunctory.

All that has changed in recent years, not least for performances of Britten's *War Requiem* in Birmingham Town Hall, and for the Verdi *Requiem*, the concluding concert in the Adrian Boult Hall, broadcast on BBC Radio 3.

On a more intimate scale, the Birmingham Conservatoire Chamber Choir, under the successive direction of David Saint, Jeffrey Skidmore and Paul Spicer, has become a major force, particularly in the performance of British chamber-choir repertoire, and in the performance of contemporary music. Its recording of choral works by Birmingham-based John Joubert, headed by his Thomas Hardy cantata *South of the Line*, was released in the spring of 2017 to universal acclaim, with an extended and enthusiastic review on BBC Radio 3.

A favoured performing venue for the Chamber Choir is the Victorian Gothic St Alban's Church, in the suburb of Highgate just south of Birmingham city centre. Its acoustic is perfectly suited to the demands for both warmth and definition, and the atmosphere of the place is immediately conducive to spiritual contemplation. It is often used for broadcasts and CD recordings, though traffic noise can be intrusive, sometimes necessitating nocturnal music-making.

Paul Spicer rehearses the Birmingham Conservatoire Chamber Choir in the Arena Foyer, an intimate space tucked beneath the Adrian Boult Hall dressing-rooms, and used for lectures, meetings, workshops and post-concert VIP receptions.

The Birmingham Conservatoire Chamber Choir performs in the High Victorian St Alban's Church in Highgate, just outside Birmingham city centre. This is an atmospheric venue both for concerts and recording.

'St Alban's acoustic is perfectly suited to the demands for both warmth and definition, and the atmosphere of the place is immediately conducive to spiritual contemplation.'

MUSIC TECHNOLOGY

What began in an empty room in Paradise Circus in the year 2000, as an offshoot of the Conservatoire's Composition Department, with only four Macintosh computers to populate it, has grown into one of the country's most renowned and successful music technology departments. Under the guidance of Lamberto Coccioli (now Associate Principal of the Conservatoire), the department developed to such an extent that now Music Technology is offered as a principal study at both undergraduate and post-graduate level, with PhD students undertaking research projects.

Simon Hall, Head of the Department, explains further:

'The study of Music Technology is usually concerned with the artistic use of technology for creation, capture, manipulation and reproduction of music. We live at that particular intersection between arts and science which is a particularly exciting and creative place to occupy.

'In addition to its own creativity, the Music Technology Department also supports the wider Conservatoire mission. All students have access to our facilities, and we work very closely on projects with the Composition, Jazz and Performance Departments. To share a building with six hundred trainee professional performers affords countless opportunities for collaboration, and our students get a lot of practice in working with colleagues from other departments on creative production, music to picture, live electronics and recording projects.'

Alumni are now working in roles that range from senior staff in specialist equipment companies such as Apple and Audient, through to broadcasters such as the BBC, Channel 4 and Sky. And credits include work with Matthew Bourne's New Adventures dance company, Glastonbury, the Royal Shakespeare Company and West End theatres, and artists Madonna, Robbie Williams and Coldplay.

Now comfortably at home in Birmingham Conservatoire's new home, the Music Technology Department can feel it has a finger on every pulse. As Julian Lloyd Webber has told me, every practice room is primed with digital facilities, and can be streamed in real time to anywhere in the world.

Those students on the fourth-floor practice rooms in Paradise Circus in the olden days would be amazed.

Students putting their music technology training into practice.

BRASS

Students of brass instruments have long gone on to great success in the country's major orchestras, whether as members of full-time symphony orchestras or as freelancers lending their strengths to part-time ensembles. Tutors bring their own performing experience to their coaching.

RIGHT AND FOLLOWING PAGES
At the Conservatoire, students have the choice of both orchestral and brass band instruments. There are various masterclasses available, and students also have access to bespoke classes aimed at helping them with both their individual performance and their skills playing as part of an ensemble.

MASTERCLASS

The Swedish trumpeter Håkan Hardenberger, one of the best performers on the instrument in the world, gives a masterclass to students at the Conservatoire, taking a brass quintet through its paces.

ORCHESTRA

Most of the tutors are performers themselves in the highest-quality orchestras around the world, and students soon learn to perform comfortably in ensembles of various sizes. The CBSO mentoring scheme brings obvious rewards, as the young players take back to the Conservatoire the experience they have gained sitting alongside CBSO players in rehearsal under some of the world's greatest conductors.

The Birmingham Philharmonic Orchestra collaborates with Conservatoire students participating in the John Ludlow Concerto Competition.

VOCALS

The vocal offering ranges from operatic presentation through the various solo song genres, and on into choral music in all its styles. Public performance and commercial recordings feature largely in the student activities, with tutors, as in every other department, bringing their own vast professional expertise.

LEFT AND FOLLOWING PAGES
Birmingham Conservatoire boasts singers adept in all kinds of repertoire, from grand opera, through Lieder, and on to folk music and jazz.

OPPOSITE *Catherine Foster (pictured singing left) enrolled at Birmingham Conservatoire at a time when she was still active as a midwife back home in Nottingham. She has risen to become one of the world's great Wagnerian and Straussian sopranos, and sang Brunnhilde at the Bayreuth Festival's Ring Cycle every year between 2013–17.*

JAZZ

Although jazz came comparatively late to the syllabus of the School of Music/Conservatoire, it has proved one of the institution's most outstanding offerings. Students have access to performing opportunities in a variety of city venues (including pre-concert gigs in the main bar at Symphony Hall), and benefit from masterclasses given by a range of visitors.

A double-bass player, completely immersed in his performance, poised for playing pizzicato (plucking the strings of the instrument).

RIGHT AND OVERLEAF Jazz students at the Conservatoire are able to perform in a variety of venues, from local venues to international festivals, and have the freedom to explore their own unique styles and sounds.

OPPOSITE *Jazzlines is a programme of creative jazz music, an initiative shared in collaboration with Birmingham Town Hall and Symphony Hall. It encourages new talent, offering opportunities and support for jazz musicians.*

Ronnie Scott's opened on Birmingham Broad Street around the same time as Symphony Hall in 1991. It was an offshoot of the famous club in London, and gave performance opportunities to Conservatoire jazz students. It closed down in 2002 and the premises were subsequently taken over by a comedy club, and latterly a lap-dancing club.

World famous drummer Elvin Jones, who left a lasting impression on jazz drumming, performing at Ronnie Scott's Birmingham in 2001. Then in his seventies, he also gave a masterclass to jazz students at the Conservatoire that year.

STRINGS

The String Department was traditionally the strongest section at the Birmingham School of Music. Now at the Conservatoire, the strings have been joined by the other instrumental sections, and together they contribute to success in both orchestral and chamber music.

From orchestral instruments through to guitar, the Conservatoire String Department covers it all.

Harp tuition at the
Conservatoire does not
only include the familiar
47-stringed, 7-pedalled
instrument. Here we have
an attractive example of
the Celtic harp.

WIND

Wind tuition covers the needs of orchestral players, band-playing (brass band and big band included) and solo performers. Graduates can often be found among the ranks of well-established orchestras, whether operatic, symphony or chamber, and the department was enhanced in 2016 by the arrival of Sir James and Lady Jeanne Galway as visiting flute tutors.

OPPOSITE A student pauses during a break in her performance on a bassoon.

ABOVE Lady Jeanne Galway takes a flute masterclass.

Stockhausen's Der Kleine Harlekin requires more than just musical expertise from the clarinet player, who must also dance and mime while performing.

FOLK MUSIC

Study at the Conservatoire covers a huge variety of styles, from world music (such as the Conservatoire's famous Indonesian gamelan and Indian raga) to the native music indigenous to European countries. Conservatoire folk musicians are often easily able to take their offerings out into the world beyond the home building.

OPPOSITE Folk ensemble The Destroyers perform at City of Sounds: Destruction Party, a celebratory send off for the Adrian Boult Hall in 2016.

RECOLLECTIONS

Margaret Cotterill

1940s/1950s

When I was fourteen, my parents decided that I needed professional piano tuition, as until then I had been taught by a lady who lived across the road. The Birmingham School of Music was recommended and an interview was duly arranged. Going into Birmingham was in itself a big event for me, as well as being nervous at the prospect of an interview.

Even though I was not alone, I entered the huge building with great trepidation, being quite overwhelmed by its size and formality. I remember giant pillars, impressive staircases and marble floors. The surroundings were so austere it was scary.

My parents and I were taken up the stairs and ushered into the office of Dr Christopher Edmunds, the Principal. He had a lovely smile, which creased up all his face until his twinkling, kind eyes were all you noticed. He was most welcoming, shaking hands with each of us and addressing us by name. He seemed really pleased to meet us.

As he talked, telling us about BSM, I began to relax, because he had a soothing, reassuring voice, until he suggested that we should meet the teacher

Miss Vera K. Smith. Miss Smith found us some rickety chairs, from other rooms. She talked to us about her teaching philosophy before asking me to play to her. I probably played Durand's First Waltz, as this was highly rated by my teacher.

Finally, Miss Smith said that she would like to teach me, as she could see that I had potential, but that I would need to practise diligently and carefully, because there were many technical faults that I would need to overcome, before she would be able to enter me for exams.

Many of the staff were professional concert performers, well known and loved by audiences. We students would try to catch a glimpse of them and talk in hushed tones when they appeared. Some names I recall are Tom Bromley, David Willcocks, Lilian Niblette and Lena Wood: these in the later 1940s.

Attitudes to teachers were different in those post-war days from nowadays. They were treated with great deference, looked up to almost like gods, so a word of praise from them was almost like being presented with a medal, it was so highly prized. Most teachers had very kind hearts and were genuinely fond of their pupils. Past students still talk of their teachers with great affection.

I was later able to tell Vera K. that she would have me as a pupil for much longer, as I was applying for a place on the new Teachers' Training Diploma course that was starting in September. She was overjoyed. From my understanding, this must have been the first course, over two years, for full-time students that the BSM offered.

There was a large common room with a motley assortment of furniture – old sagging settees, upright chairs, various large and smaller tables, all very second-hand and several dilapidated, old carpets, but we came to love it – it was our sanctuary! It became full of friendship and laughter. I think there were about twelve of us in the first year. Those were wonderful days as we all got on so well together.

One person, who had a heart of gold and looked after the welfare of all the students, although that was not his role, was Mr Brookes. He was the caretaker, piano tuner, general factotum and a brilliant solver of problems. If two of you suddenly decided you would like to play a piece for two pianos – no problem. In the blink of an eye, he would have manoeuvred two pianos into a suitable room. If you realised, at the last moment, that you were supposed to be rehearsing for a small concert, but had not arranged a rehearsal room – no problem – chairs and stands would appear and be arranged like magic.

Of course, a great deal of time during the day was taken up with practice. Piano, clarinet, recorders and singing all needed to be practised. We often used to have to search for practice rooms, as obviously they were in great demand. Often this meant resorting to those in the basement, which were cold, dark and dank. On one occasion I was practising my clarinet in this basement room when I realised that a mouse was just sitting there looking at me.

We organised two dinners: one at the Botanical Gardens, the other at the Plough and Harrow. Both were a sell-out, really well attended by staff and students. Specially invited guests were Sir Arthur Bliss, Clarence Raybould, Julius Harrison and of course the Principal, Chris Edmunds. Clarence Raybould, quite unexpectedly, seated himself at the piano and proceeded to entertain one and all with songs and party tricks, until everyone ached from laughing so much.

The highlight of 1954, the centenary of the Birmingham and Midland Institute, was the Celebrity Concert in the Town Hall on Wednesday, 8 December, where Anthony Pini was the cello soloist in Elgar's Concerto in E minor, which was conducted by Clarence Raybould.

Jean Sibelius sent greetings, given pride of place at the front of the programme. The concert was on his eighty-ninth birthday:

'Greetings from Jean Sibelius

'The activity of the Birmingham and Midland Institute has always been of the greatest importance for English music and for the Art of Music as a whole. For my own part, I am deeply grateful for all that the Institute has done to promote my music, particularly during the lifetime of my unforgettable friend Granville Bantock. I send the Institute on its 100th anniversary my warmest greeting hoping that it will always follow its noble traditions.'

There had been talk for many years about the possibility of founding a Junior offshoot to the Birmingham School of Music, largely spurred by murmurings from the City of Birmingham Education Department that its existence would help tick funding boxes.

But it was not until 1993, once the BSM had been recast as a Conservatoire, that this wish became a reality, and the Birmingham Junior Conservatoire was born. Its first Principal was the piano pedagogue Heather Slade-Lipkin, arriving from the illustrious Chetham's School in Manchester. That same September saw the installation of George Caird as Principal of the Conservatoire itself.

Taking advantage of the weekend lull in tuition and lectures for the population of the parent Conservatoire, the Birmingham Conservatoire Junior School, as the new enterprise was cumbersomely named (the snappier 'Junior Conservatoire' came later), took over the Paradise Circus building. Teaching rooms buzzed with instrumental and vocal lessons given on a one-to-one basis to children ranging from infant-school age to sixth form; lecture rooms were given over to tuition in A-level Music, and larger spaces resonated with the rehearsals of

Birmingham Conservatoire on a Saturday is busy with all kinds of classes going on in the Junior Conservatoire, from straightforward instrumental lessons to ensemble rehearsals.

various ensembles. End-of-term public concerts were a feature of the School's activities right from the very beginning.

And corridors and foyers throughout the building were thronged with parents doing crossword puzzles or reading, snacking out of lunchboxes, as they waited for their talented offspring to emerge from their very thorough tuition.

There were strong links between Junior and Senior Conservatoires in terms of staff, some of whom taught in both establishments, and who inculcated an ethos of preparation for progress to higher musical education.

'Interaction between Junior Conservatoire and the parent Conservatoire is particularly strong here, and central to our mission,' said Timothy English, who took over as Principal in January 2000 after a spell as Head of Strings at Oundle School. Before that he was at Hertfordshire Music Service, and had a freelance career playing violin with the Royal Philharmonic Orchestra, London Mozart Players and London Virtuosi, among others.

'Links with the other UK Junior Departments are very strong, and we meet regularly under the auspices of Conservatoires UK as the Junior Forum.'

'Corridors and foyers throughout the building were thronged with parents as they waited for their talented offspring to emerge.'

The Junior Conservatoire offers courses mostly to those between the ages of eight and eighteen, although classes are also available to children as young as three or four through the Young Strings Project, where children can start learning, for example, the violin, viola and cello.

Many opportunities are offered through the Conservatoire thanks to its partnerships with other musical and cultural programmes and organisations, both in Birmingham and beyond.

'Teaching rooms buzzed with instrumental and vocal lessons given on a one-to-one basis to children ranging from infant-school age to sixth form.'

Junior courses include classical music, jazz and chamber music. Students are encouraged to participate in performances as much as possible, including solo performances, with termly recitals and an end of year concert.

The junior courses train talented young musicians to the point where they are ready and able to move on to a senior conservatoire or music college.

RECOLLECTIONS

Duncan Honeybourne

1990s

I arrived at the Conservatoire in September 1996, after five years in the Royal Academy of Music Junior Department. It is interesting to reflect now that some of my mentors and colleagues thought Birmingham an odd choice and, indeed, some advised against it in the strongest of terms! I think – even now – there seems to be an entrenched tendency for many musicians to be rather London-centric, and to assume that the capital is the place to start a career. I had won the Junior RAM piano prize and had a place to continue at the RAM, so the decision to relocate to the Midlands seemed strange to some of my teachers and contemporaries. But I've always been one to make my own decisions, and this was one I took with steely conviction. What is more, I have never regretted it; in fact, I have always positively relished the directions in which it led me.

Admittedly, apart from purely musical considerations, two health issues played their part in my decision to look outside London. I've always been physically hampered by cerebral palsy – in my case fairly mild but nonetheless limiting – and getting around London was always difficult for me. Being on the autistic spectrum

rendered me prone to sensory overload, severe anxiety and social confusion, and the demands of the capital presented a mountain on which, even if I managed to climb it, I felt I'd struggle to flourish. But, just as significantly, Birmingham was the home town of my mother, my grandparents and many cousins. I had strong roots in the city and throughout the Midlands, a region I'd known and loved since early childhood. And the Midlands' illustrious musical heritage was well known to me, as was the region's distinguished centre of professional training, the Birmingham School of Music/Conservatoire. For me, it was an obvious and exciting choice.

In terms of the professional training on offer, Birmingham had just as strong a staff as the RAM. Just as at the Academy, there was a highly gifted keyboard faculty with a vast range of expertise and professional interests, and the body of staff across the Conservatoire boasted an immense richness and depth of specialism. Malcolm Wilson ran an inspired piano department driven by the highest professional standards and a purposeful energy. The faculty staff covered a wide range of repertoire specialisms and sympathies, their communal *raison d'être* fostering and encouraging a wide range of repertoire and placing important practical emphasis on pianistic versatility and professional self-reliance. Noteworthy staff in other departments included that great Bach scholar Stephen Daw, the remarkable musical polymath John Mayer and the ever revelatory Anthony Cross, all of whose conversation, insights and encyclopaedic knowledge were fascinating and humbling in equal measure. It is sad to reflect on the losses we have sustained in the years since, and, in addition to those three, the late Michael Hill was a decisive influence. This remarkable man displayed great personal kindness to me and shared warm encouragement and insights, most memorably into the musical world of his mentor, Edmund Rubbra. I still have a signed photograph of the great Russian pianist Benno Moiseiwitsch that Michael gave me, inscribed to former BSM piano professor Lilian Niblette, whose teaching room it once adorned. From my earliest encounters with the institution, I loved the freedom and flexibility that the Conservatoire offered, allowing one space and time to structure the course to one's own

interests and allowing time for career strands to emerge and develop naturally.

But there was another front, too, on which Birmingham won hands down for me right from the start. London is of course very spread out, with considerable distances between its cultural hotspots. Birmingham's artistic hub is central and compact, and its musical community blessed with a real community 'feel' to enliven its rich and ever present past heritage and present 'buzz'. With my physical disability, everything was more accessible; I'd easily be able to commute from my new family base in Worcestershire; I'd be working in my 'family city', and I'd have a fabulous opportunity to lay the foundations of my career in a city and region with a fabulously integrated and vibrant musical platform.

And so it proved. I had a wonderful range of opportunities in Birmingham, which I'm sure would have been much more fragmented and difficult to obtain elsewhere. I gave masses of recitals in Birmingham, throughout the Midlands, and elsewhere, gaining lots of invaluable experience and sowing the seeds of a career in the process. I built up a sizeable network of engagements with Midlands music clubs, concerto dates with local orchestras, and much chamber music with professional colleagues as well as fellow students, and I had the chance to broadcast recitals from Birmingham on BBC local radio, experience that definitely wouldn't have happened in London! Throughout my student years I gave regular recitals in the Friday lunchtime series at St Philip's Cathedral, including piano-duet recitals with Assistant Head of Keyboard John Humphreys. These cathedral concerts gave me a terrific opportunity to devise and build interesting programmes for a regular and loyal audience, with many of my repertoire choices from the outset focusing on British music and unusual repertoire. This really harnessed interests and aspirations that have gone on to be long-term cornerstones of my musical life, not least in running my own lunchtime concert series in Dorset in later years. I also appreciated the flexibility within the college's curriculum, something that prepared me well for the life of a musician in the twenty-first century. I was able to take second-study organ, with Marcus Huxley at St Philip's and David Saint at St Chad's Cathedrals, and to hold a parish organ post in Worcestershire, where I gave some organ recitals. This too has continued to be a cherished and enriching ingredient of my ongoing career.

The most memorable and significant single concert experience of my time at the Conservatoire came during my third undergraduate year, as part of the joint orchestral project the Conservatoire mounted with the Royal Irish Academy of Music, in commemoration of the RIAM's 150th birthday. I was asked to play the wonderful Mozart Concerto for Two Pianos with Dublin pianist Finghin Collins at Birmingham's Symphony Hall and Dublin's National Concert Hall, in two concerts also broadcast on radio and television. Not only was this an enormous honour and a joyous experience of music-making, but it also marked the beginning of several ongoing associations. I was invited back to Dublin to give a recital and subsequently became a regular visitor to that wonderful country, playing throughout Ireland and establishing many friendships and links there over the best part of twenty years. All thanks to the Conservatoire! Following this appearance, the Conservatoire sent me around the country to give various recitals, one of them in the Turner Sims Concert Hall at the University of Southampton where – little did I know then – I would join the staff fifteen years later!

The Midlands' own rich musical heritage has also played a big part in my performing career. I've always been interested in neglected byways of the repertoire, as well as in promoting living composers, and I've delved into a good amount of music by Midland composers. Many of these have had BSM/BC associations. One of the most important composer associations of my life was established at the Conservatoire, namely my friendship and collaboration with Andrew Downes. I first encountered Andrew's music as a student, and I first played the Piano Sonata No. 1 at the Three Choirs Festival in Hereford. I also made my first BBC Radio 3 appearance playing the Downes Sonatina for Piano, in a programme recorded at the Conservatoire's Recital Hall. Andrew went on to write several more piano works for me, including a piano concerto, which I premiered at the Town Hall in 2009, and I've recently made a two-disc set for EMI Records of his complete solo piano music. I'm also proud to have premiered the Third Piano Sonata of John Joubert, another former BSM staff member, and two sonatas by Richard Francis, a former student. Birmingham is crucial to my musical identity and some of the music I've gone on to champion and love has its roots there too.

My time at the Conservatoire wasn't always easy, for my autism-spectrum disorder and related health problems caught up with me while there and I suffered a breakdown that could have ended my studies entirely. But I had some excellent support and was shown great kindness and understanding, for which I shall always be grateful. The human framework within the place certainly helped me back onto my feet, and forward into my career.

It's difficult to separate my Conservatoire-specific experiences from the wider musical richness of my studentship and apprenticeship in Birmingham. That's how it should be, of course,

and my time there did exactly what a positive student experience should do: it replicated, in numerous aspects, the professional life that would follow it, giving me fabulous opportunities to spread my wings, experiment, make mistakes, grow and develop. And in so many ways it prepared the ground for what was to come. Not only did I do masses of solo and chamber music playing in mainstream repertoire, but I explored and devised programmes featuring unusual works, something that has been a central focus of my work since. I gave lecture recitals, gained valuable teaching experience and played regularly for other students' exams, staying on after graduation as a staff pianist. This fed directly into so much that I've done on an almost daily basis ever since in my work in music education.

Although the majority of my career has unfolded since I left Birmingham, and most of it far away from the city, the place is still crucial to my identity and development as a musician. I'm proud that it's where my career began, and I treasure my affiliation with the city's – and the region's – great musical and artistic heritage. I shall watch the latest exciting developments in the Conservatoire's historical narrative with immense interest, excitement and pleasure.

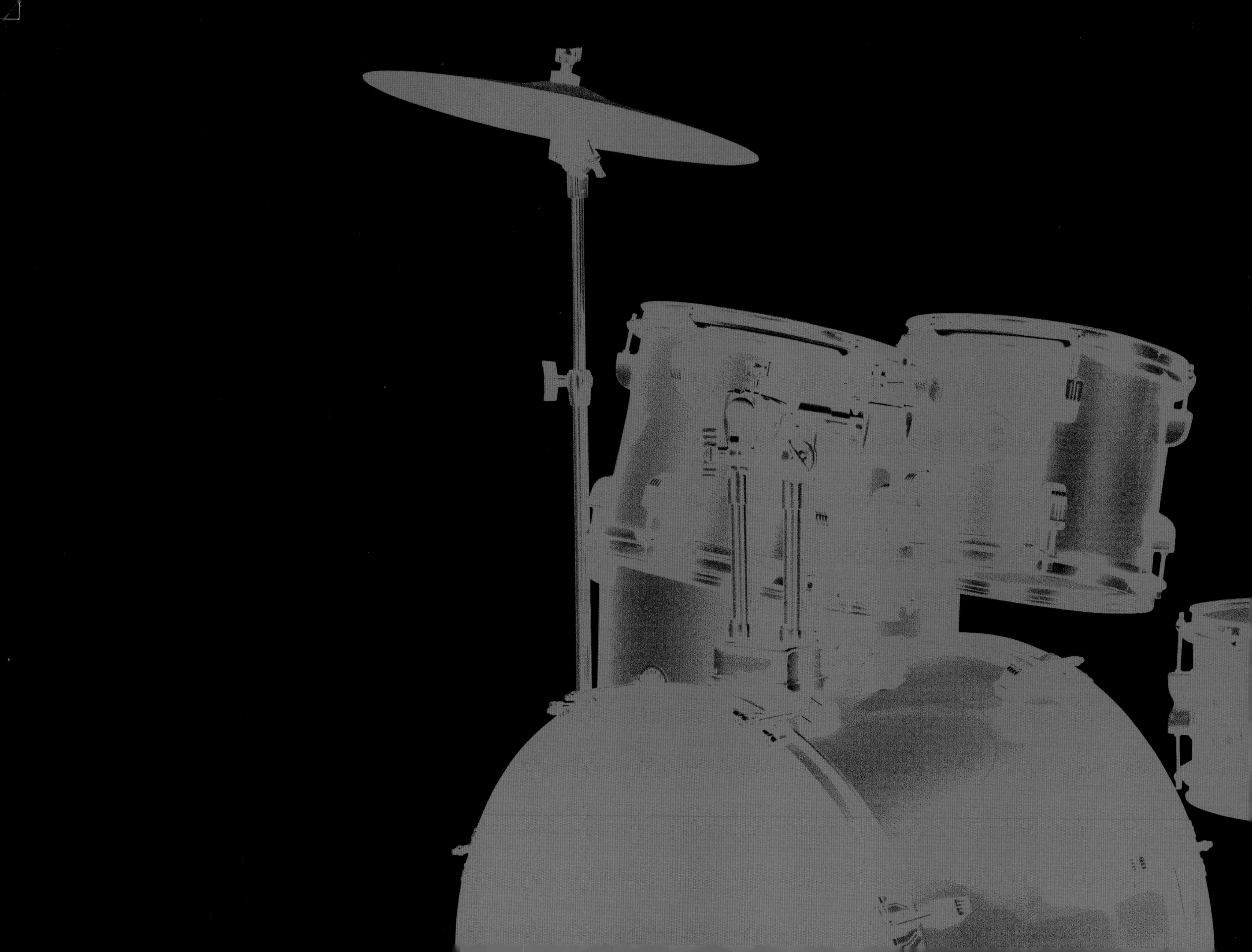

The amateur dabblers who enrolled in what was to become the Penny Class in Elementary Singing at the Birmingham and Midland Institute in 1859 would probably not have the capacity to be dazzled by what is nowadays on offer to the students of what has grown to become a renowned international conservatoire.

All manner of facilities and subject areas are available, opportunities that were unimaginable over a century and a half ago, and opportunities that give the individual student the capacity virtually to tailor their studies to their own requirements and projected career aspirations.

One staff member concluded some years ago that no fewer than fifty-two skills were required from someone planning to enter the music profession as a freelance; the number may well have risen since. Among these skills were listed facility in information technology, marketing, accounting, presentation both personally and on the stage, a high standard of literacy, an ability to network, acknowledge of how to navigate transport systems, a tongue for languages, diary organisation, and all sorts of other desiderata even before one starts to consider musical ability.

The Conservatoire's professional development programme paves the way for the student to acquire this career portfolio. It also offers the chance to build connections with a wealth of musical organisations, including the CBSO, Welsh National Opera, Birmingham Contemporary Music Group, Jazzlines, Tredegar Town Band, Ex Cathedra, the Royal Shakespeare Company, Birmingham Royal Ballet, Orchestra of the Swan, Town Hall and Symphony Hall, Birmingham Music Service, and more. And it recommends that undergraduates during their third year study at one of the Conservatoire's partner institutions in Europe or the USA, links that have come about through such schemes as Erasmus, among others.

Students have the opportunity to rehearse and perform in such prestigious venues as Birmingham Town Hall, Symphony Hall, the CBSO Centre, Birmingham Cathedral and St Chad's Cathedral – all of this in addition to the state-of-the-art performing venues within the new Conservatoire building itself.

One aspect of the Conservatoire's syllabus that our ancestors in 1859 could scarcely have dreamed about is the Performance Coaching programme, the first of its kind in the UK, which applies the principles of sports psychology to elite musical performance. The programme was largely the brainchild of the late Karen O'Connor, oboist with the CBSO and

Conservatoire students performing at the Beijing Modern Music Festival in China in 2016.

'All manner of facilities and subject areas are available now, opportunities that were unimaginable over a century and a half ago.'

The Beijing Modern Music Festival is an influential contemporary music event, providing an important platform for young musicians around the world.

Conservatoire tutor, who was able to talk both colleagues and students through their pre-performance nerves.

And those Penny Singers could never have conceived of a course offering a BMus honours degree in Jazz, a style of music that hadn't even been invented in the mid-nineteenth century. All the tutors are active professional performers and composers. Students organise regular performances at venues around the city, as well as having the opportunity to perform at leading jazz festivals, such as Cheltenham. They also benefit from masterclasses given by leading performers and composers of the day, and are able to take part in the Conservatoire's Live Jazz Broadcast series.

Then there is the dynamic Music Technology course, aimed at creating multi-skilled and versatile graduates who can use technology to create, perform and distribute music. The business is fast-evolving, and students are trained to acquire a firm understanding of all the developing processes involved. The Conservatoire's new home is equipped with state-of the-art facilities in dedicated venues around the building, including seven industry-standard recording studios and a black-box theatre for experimental performance projects, and the course

is organised in conjunction with Birmingham City University's Faculty of Computing, Engineering and the Built Environment.

Whatever the course of study, once having obtained a BMus degree, alumni have the option of pursuing a postgraduate course. The programmes offer a huge range of qualifications across every discipline, from performance to musicology, and there is in addition a post-Masters performance course, the Advanced Postgraduate Diploma, which is available in six specialist areas: Instrumental Performance, Vocal Performance, Collaborative Piano, Opera Répétiteur, Chamber Music Performance or Choral Conducting.

This blossoming of opportunity for students of Birmingham Conservatoire is light years away from anything aspired to in 1859, when the Birmingham and Midland Institute first launched those elementary singing classes. It was a case of the genie being let out of the bottle, and the eventual, long-festering result was tension between the BMI and the burgeoning School of Music.

OPPOSITE Conservatoire students performing at Birmingham's Mailbox, previously the GPO sorting office and now a high-class shopping and dining mall, as well as home to BBC WM.

RIGHT The Jazz Department's recently formed Ellington Orchestra performing at its launch gig 'Duke Ellington: We Love You Madly' at the Town Hall in February 2017.

But since that long-drawn-out divorce has been accomplished, with the Conservatoire now a major part of Birmingham City University, relations between the Conservatoire and the BMI have become far easier, cordial and productive. It should be put on record that the BMI building in Birmingham's Margaret Street provided a teaching home for the Conservatoire's Keyboard Department during the final stage of the Paradise Circus demolition, and that there are the plans for the two institutions to continue to work closely in this beneficial relationship.

From September 2017, the Conservatoire has reinvented itself as not only the digital conservatoire of the future, but also a multidisciplinary institution, completing a merger with Birmingham School of Acting (another part of Birmingham City University with a long and impressive history).

The move combined two schools of such high repute (according to the Guardian University Guide rankings 2018) that, as of the time of merging, Birmingham Conservatoire could be considered the highest ranking multidisciplinary conservatoire in the UK.

The future is bright for this combined institution, and opportunities to collaborate – which have always taken place internally – will become regular, plentiful and accessible. With both disciplines joining together on the same campus under the name Birmingham Conservatoire, two vibrant communities will create an impressive single force of creative energy – a positive and necessary step to take this institution into the future.

Penny Singing classes? Now a studentship at Birmingham Conservatoire can put the world at a graduate's feet.

I arrived at Birmingham Conservatoire in 1993 to study piano performance, and my original impression of the building was very modern; the facility was well equipped for a conservatoire, and the teachers and staff were very friendly.

Birmingham Conservatoire perhaps was not every music student's first choice in those days, but students who did come to study at the Conservatoire were passionate about music and very keen to learn. Staff were helpful and flexible; the relationship between tutors and students in general was smooth and close. To me, its open-minded mentality and fair treatment to all students – including international students – made the Conservatoire so special. Since I first joined, the biggest change, perhaps, has been in the tutors, lecturers and staff. More artists from international backgrounds or the younger generation joined the Conservatoire, which no doubt created a fresh and exciting atmosphere and raised the standard. Located in the city centre, the outer appearance of the building was a bit blank, although the atmosphere within was lively and vigorous.

The Conservatoire's reputation grew rapidly – locally and internationally – when I left England in 2001. Instead of choosing a music college with a 'Royal' title, perhaps in London, more and more 'first-class' musicians from all over the world choose to study at the Birmingham Conservatoire.

I personally was offered opportunities to lecture on the aesthetics of music, and to work as an overseas recruiting agent while I was a PhD student in Musicology at the Conservatoire, which helped to develop my own career tremendously, both academically and administratively. I was offered a full-time position as an assistant professor at the National Sun Yat-Sen University in Taiwan as soon as I got my PhD, and I was very honoured to receive the Honorary Fellowship of Birmingham Conservatoire in 2015. I received my professorship about a year ago and now work at the National Taiwan University of Arts.

To me, Birmingham Conservatoire is not only the college where I studied and got my Music Performance Diploma, MA and PhD degrees; as an international student, it also provided me with a rich learning environment, great opportunities to connect and a fair chance to work. The memory of those beautiful and exciting days at the Birmingham Conservatoire stays with me. It really changed my life!

David Wynne

2010s

When I auditioned for my MMus in the Vocal Department of Birmingham Conservatoire, to start in September 2012, my first impression was of a really friendly, warm and encouraging building. There was a sense of 'putting people at ease' for the audition process, which started right from the moment you walked into the reception, through the warm-up and into the actual audition. While it felt like a place of hard work, talent and success, it also seemed to be a place of encouragement, enjoyment and of care – I was right.

Although I had come to do a master's degree in singing, I had previously studied elsewhere as a trumpeter. I found the standard of singers to be exceptionally high and the staff to be of an excellent calibre too. I was fortunate to study with Henry Herford, a world-renowned baritone, and then to receive a scholarship to study conducting with influential conductor Paul Spicer.

While training to be a singer at the Conservatoire it was choral conducting that I loved most, and it was through the continued support and guidance from Paul Spicer that my career as a choral conductor grew. I now run two choral societies, the historic Birmingham Festival Choral Society and the Ryton Chorale. I also teach at the Birmingham Junior Conservatoire, where I run three of the four choirs, as well as teaching singing, conducting and aural training. I work for the Welsh National Opera and also co-run a music education charity based at St Chad's Cathedral in Birmingham.

Following my time as a student at the Conservatoire, as a teacher in the Junior Department I have seen, and am seeing, many changes, mainly the demolition of the Adrian Boult Hall and the move to the new building. During this time I think there has been even more collaboration, certainly within the Junior Department, with everyone working together to get the best possible results and performances. There has been a real sense of excitement and anticipation from students and staff alike to start the next year in the new building. In my opinion – possibly not shared by everyone – the old building itself was not particularly attractive: a Brutalist concrete structure. Yet inside, the constant and eclectic buzz and the sounds of some of the country's most talented musicians performing and rehearsing were quite the opposite.

I read recently that the Conservatoire was ranked as fifth out of eighty-one universities, conservatoires and other higher education institutions to offer courses in music, and I have to say I am not surprised. There is an excellent combination of talent and hard work from staff and students alike, with a sense of care, support and community that make the Conservatoire a great place to work and study.

TIMELINE

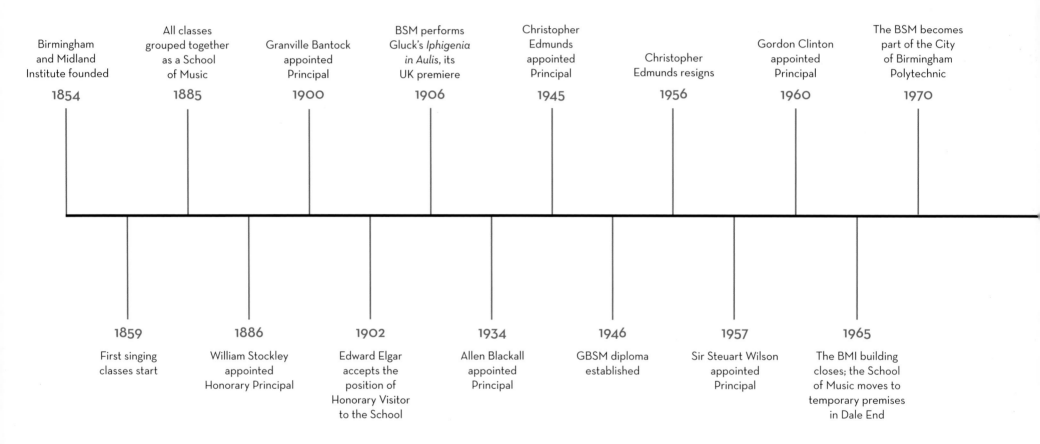

1854
Birmingham and Midland Institute founded

1885
All classes grouped together as a School of Music

1900
Granville Bantock appointed Principal

1906
BSM performs Gluck's *Iphigenia in Aulis*, its UK premiere

1945
Christopher Edmunds appointed Principal

1956
Christopher Edmunds resigns

1960
Gordon Clinton appointed Principal

1970
The BSM becomes part of the City of Birmingham Polytechnic

1859
First singing classes start

1886
William Stockley appointed Honorary Principal

1902
Edward Elgar accepts the position of Honorary Visitor to the School

1934
Allen Blackall appointed Principal

1946
GBSM diploma established

1957
Sir Steuart Wilson appointed Principal

1965
The BMI building closes; the School of Music moves to temporary premises in Dale End

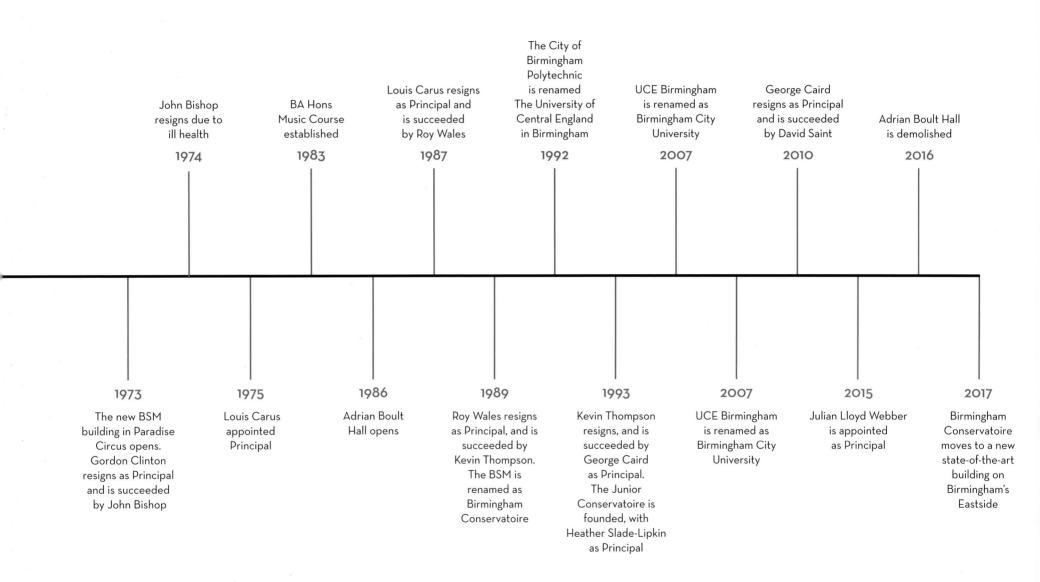

John Bishop
resigns due to
ill health

1974

BA Hons
Music Course
established

1983

Louis Carus resigns
as Principal and
is succeeded
by Roy Wales

1987

The City of
Birmingham
Polytechnic
is renamed
The University of
Central England
in Birmingham

1992

UCE Birmingham
is renamed as
Birmingham City
University

2007

George Caird
resigns as Principal
and is succeeded
by David Saint

2010

Adrian Boult Hall
is demolished

2016

1973

The new BSM
building in Paradise
Circus opens.
Gordon Clinton
resigns as Principal
and is succeeded
by John Bishop

1975

Louis Carus
appointed
Principal

1986

Adrian Boult
Hall opens

1989

Roy Wales resigns
as Principal, and is
succeeded by
Kevin Thompson.
The BSM is
renamed as
Birmingham
Conservatoire

1993

Kevin Thompson
resigns, and is
succeeded by
George Caird
as Principal.
The Junior
Conservatoire is
founded, with
Heather Slade-Lipkin
as Principal

2007

UCE Birmingham
is renamed as
Birmingham City
University

2015

Julian Lloyd Webber
is appointed
as Principal

2017

Birmingham
Conservatoire
moves to a new
state-of-the-art
building on
Birmingham's
Eastside

ACKNOWLEDGEMENTS

In preparing this book I sent out a questionnaire to students and staff from across the decades. I would like to express my thanks to all who responded, and to all those students and staff, past and present, with whom I have had illuminating conversations, anxious to share their reminiscences and observations with me. I would also like to acknowledge the interest shown by past Principals with whom I have personally had the pleasure of working: Roy Wales, Kevin Thompson, George Caird, David Saint, and now Julian Lloyd Webber. Philip Fisher, administrator of the Birmingham and Midland Institute, has been friendly and generous with his help, and it is thanks to the squirrelling undertaken by his library staff that I have been able to present here the ground plans of the original School of Music premises.

The Birmingham Conservatoire Association (much more than an amazing old boys' and girls' club) has been so helpful, especially two of its guiding lights, Helen Mills and Jeremy Patterson. I would also like to remember here Peter Ward, one of the BCA's founding fathers, who passed away at a great age just as this book was being completed. But even more valuable than these has been the unstinting assistance of John Smith, archivist of the BCA, who has responded with enthusiasm and promptitude to every query, and whose massive 300-page tome chronicling all the minutiae of the activities of the Birmingham School of Music and Birmingham Conservatoire has engrossed me and put me eternally in his debt.

SOURCES

I have consulted many printed sources, both books and newspaper archives, during the writing of this history, among which the following have been the most prominent:

Birmingham School of Music 1985-1986 Centenary Year souvenir programme (City of Birmingham Polytechnic, 1985)

Brock, David, *The Birmingham School of Music: Its First Century* (City of Birmingham Polytechnic 1986)

Downes, Frank, *Around the Horn* (Birmingham City Council, 1994)

Fanfare, Birmingham Conservatoire Association magazine

Handford, Margaret, *Sounds Unlikely: Music in Birmingham* (Studley: Brewin Books, 2006)

Smith, John, *Notes on the History of Birmingham Conservatoire* (unpublished)

Stewart, Margaret, *English Singer* (London: Duckworth, 1970)

Sutcliffe Smith, John, *The Story of Music in Birmingham* (Birmingham: Cornish Brothers Limited, 1945)

Waterhouse, Rachel E., *The Birmingham and Midland Institute 1854-1954* (Birmingham: Birmingham & Midland Institute, 1954)

INDEX

ABOUT THE AUTHOR

Christopher Morley is a product of the Second World War, as a result of his father serving in the British Army and meeting a beautiful young woman in Naples. Their first date was a performance of Boito's *Mefistofele* at the San Carlo opera house, and the die was obviously cast.

Christopher was born and educated in Brighton, and it was a visit as a schoolboy to a rehearsal at Glyndebourne of Mozart's *Idomeneo* in 1964 that made him realise that he had to have a life in music. A three-week course in Salzburg in the next year confirmed it, and in 1966 he was admitted to the Music Department of the University of Birmingham on an Open Entrance Scholarship, under the inspiring Professorship of Anthony Lewis.

Upon graduating with Honours in 1969 he took up a career as a schoolteacher, serving as Head of Music in schools in Walsall, Edgbaston and Halesowen. In the same year he was invited to write his first review for the *Birmingham Post*, and in 1988, having escaped from the classroom, he was appointed chief music critic to the newspaper. This, regrettably, brought to an end his conducting activities with various amateur organisations, though he has dusted down his baton for a few occasions since. Today, Christopher also writes for *Musical Opinion*, *Classical Music* and *Opera*, as well as contributing broadcasts to BBC Radio 3.

Also in 1988 Christopher began teaching at Birmingham School of Music, at first in a small way, tutoring small groups of students in 'Paperwork', but later lecturing in music history, performance practice, harmony and counterpoint, and aural training, as well as liberal studies. He also ran a class in music journalism and criticism, many of whose alumni went on to make an impact as music journalists and critics, both in the UK and in Sweden. He was awarded an Honorary Fellowship in 2002, and retired from the Conservatoire in 2010.

During the course of his musical writing he has accepted invitations from all over Europe, as well as from Russia and Japan, where he was invited in 2017 to assess the country's symphony orchestras with a Western critic's ears. He also gives talks to music societies all over the UK.

Away from music, Christopher Morley loves cricket, Brighton and Hove Albion, local history, books – and cannot escape the tyranny of his cats.